# The 52 – Worcestershire's Forgotten
## First-Class Cricketers
### *by Tim Jones*

## This is number 50 of a limited edition of 52 copies

**Tim Jones**                                             **John Chadd**

# The 52

## Worcestershire's Forgotten First-Class Cricketers

By

Tim Jones

Grosvenor House
Publishing Limited

This book is published by
Grosvenor House Publishing Ltd
Link House
140 The Broadway, Tolworth, Surrey, KT6 7HT.
www.grosvenorhousepublishing.co.uk

A CIP record for this book
is available from the British Library

ISBN 978-1-83975-584-2

# Dedication

To my brother Jonathan, the kindest
and most honest of all gentlemen.

# Foreword by John Chadd

When Tim asked me if I would write a foreword to his book I was both honoured and surprised. It occurred to me then that I might have been asked because I was possibly the oldest living member of his '52' club. I certainly have had a long association with Worcestershire CCC.

As a schoolboy in the late-1940s I used to cycle from Hereford to Worcester, parking my bike under the old pavilion. There was no need to lock your cycle in those days. Hereford to Worcester was a hilly road and you had to cope with Fromes Hill, The Malverns or Bromyard Downs, depending on which route you took and the old Sturmey Archer three-speed did not compare with the cycle gears of today. I would then watch my heroes of that era – Reg Perks, Dick Howorth, Eddie Cooper, Roly Jenkins and the rest of that team.

I was very intrigued with Tim's project because books written about sportsmen or women are normally about those who have made it to the top rather than those who for many reasons failed to achieve all their ambitions in their chosen sport.

In the mid-1950s I had two seasons as a junior professional at New Road. At that time there were about eight or 10 of us, mostly in our early twenties with the majority of us having recently completed our national service. All were talented cricketers who had come to the County's notice through their performances in league and club cricket. It was generally a good life being a young professional on the Worcestershire staff.

For one thing, we could not believe our luck in being paid for what most of us loved doing most – playing cricket! We also felt very fortunate in being able to play on one of the most beautiful grounds, not only in this country but probably in the world. It was a full and varied life, too. When the first team was playing at home, if you were a bowler you might be required to bowl a few overs at the visiting batsmen.

What a thrill it was to bowl to great players such as Colin Cowdrey, Ted Dexter and Tom Graveney, who of course was a Gloucestershire player at that time. On various occasions I was also detailed to score for the first team, do a spell of commentating on the local hospital radio or act as 12th man for the first team. One of the most important jobs the 12th man had was to get the fast bowlers their pints of beer at lunchtime and close of play.

Physical fitness was important but it was not taken nearly as seriously as it is today. If rain ruled out practice in the nets and the coach thought we needed some physical exercise we were sometimes sent up to the Brine Baths at Droitwich for a gentle dip in the warm waters there. Bowlers, especially the quicker ones were not expected to dive full length in the field. At the close of play both senior and junior players were encouraged to meet together for a drink and a chat in the bar. These were occasions when the junior players learned as much as they ever learned on the field.

After I left the staff to join the family business in 1956, I did not see very much cricket at New Road as I was playing cricket for Hereford CC at the weekend and often in the week, too. I became involved with the County again when I joined the General Committee in 1978 and enjoyed watching some great batsmen at New Road such as Glenn Turner, Graeme Hick and Tom Moody, to name just a few. And, of course, the many fine bowlers of that period.

It was the ambition of many of 'The 52' featured in this book to become established members of the Worcestershire CCC first team. Obviously, none of them for various reasons fulfilled this ambition, but many became top performers in other fields. It may have been in the professions, in business, in the media, on the stage, in the armed forces or in one of several other callings. When their hopes of first-class cricket ended it may have seemed at the time like the end of the world. But for many it was just the beginning!

# Preface

In 2005, Worcestershire County Cricket Club replaced the awarding of a county cap with a colours system for players who represent the Club in County Championship matches. When colours and numbers were allocated retrospectively to former players, 52 of them missed out because the game/s they played, while first-class, were not in the County Championship.

I feel a sense of injustice for these players, so this 'Who's Who' provides me with the opportunity to right the wrong and acknowledge the contribution of 'The 52' who, otherwise, are in danger of being air-brushed out of the Club's history.

Despite, in some instances, playing just one game, these players deserve the recognition they warrant. Their careers and lives are now celebrated and sit, with equal status, alongside the greats of Worcestershire cricket.

This book provides the opportunity to share my knowledge and, using material from my archive, also allows me to tell the stories of 'The 52' on a personal level. As well as bridging gaps and correcting inaccuracies in some existing records, I have included photographs of all 52 players plus testimonies and recollections from 16 of the 17 surviving players. There are also numerous contributions from the families of those players no longer alive, making this a definitive piece of work, a must read for any Worcestershire follower.

# Acknowledgements

I have been amazed at the number of people who have been able to help me in my quest to uncover a wealth of information about a group of players whose story has been waiting to be told for many years; they all have my heartfelt thanks.

Firstly, my thanks to Grosvenor House Publishing for their help, guidance and support in helping to produce a first-rate publication.

My good friends and fellow members at Worcestershire CCC, Jeremy Turner, Richard Brown, Mark Ashbourne, Andrew Thomas and Ross Fletcher, have all freely given their time to help in so many different ways.

Experts in their field such as Roger Mann, the great cricket historian, who has mentored and guided me over many years and always comes up with the right answer to any conundrum I throw his way. Local experts such as Terry Church who has an encyclopaedic knowledge of Black Country sportsmen, Andy Murtagh and Robert Leachman, whose knowledge of Malvern College is second to none, and Jim Morris, for so long the scorer for Herefordshire CCC, for helping to establish contact with some of the players in question. Thanks, too, to Daryl Mitchell, for providing an insight into the selection of Nick Compton to play as a 'guest'.

Many of the universities and schools around the country have provided some of the outstanding photographs you see in the book. Coupled with that, I'm grateful for their help in never giving up in the search for the information I seek. Especially: Hannah Robertson (Oriel College, Oxford); Judith Curthoys (Christ Church, Oxford); Alex Browne (Trinity Hall, Cambridge); David Chapman and Jacqueline Cox from Cambridge University); Charlotte Berry (Magdalen College, Oxford); Helen Sumping

(Brasenose College, Oxford); Flora Chatt (Bodleian Library); Nina Challenor (Tonbridge School); Toby Parker (Haileybury School); Tace Fox (Harrow School); John Paddock (Mercian Regiment Museum, Worcestershire).

During my research, it appeared that brewing had a connection to two of the players and my thanks are extended to the experts in that field who helped supply such detailed information and some outstanding accompanying pictures: Keith Osborne and Ken Smith (Brewery 'Delver'), and David Lands. Mick Cooke – another Worcestershire CCC member – was a great source of information in connection with railway history as was Andrew Jones from the Great Western Railway.

Other sources of expert help have been: The Australian War Memorial Research Centre; The Tasmanian Library; Royal Military College, Sandhurst; Pam McNicol (Stirling Council Archives), who found some wonderful photos of Thomas Sheppard; Dave Lands from the McCord Museum in Canada; and the RAF Museum.

My many friends within the cricket world have been more than willing to share information about players who have represented their county or league team. They are: Peter Radburn (Kidderminster CC); the Sussex CCC Foundation; Keith Walmsley and Mike Williams (Warwickshire CCC); Dave Griffin (Derbyshire CCC); Malcolm Eustace (Moseley CC); Dave Robinson (Coventry and North Warwick CC); David Talbot; Harry Watton; plus Mark Thornycroft; Richard, the 30th Chief of the Carmichael Clan; Graham Williams; and Richard Symonds.

Hearing the stories first-hand from the players involved has helped capture unique and priceless moments in their careers, so my gratitude goes especially to them: Brian Barrett, Alan Brown, Dennis Good, Brian Hall, Derek Isles, Brian and Karl Krikken, Simon Kimber, Amjad Mohammed, Harshad Patel, James Ralph,

Ian Rutherford, Mike Scothern, John Spilsbury, Will Thomas and Steve Watkins.

The families of those players no longer alive have taken delight in recalling the lives of their loved ones. Without the help of Angus Bell in Canada I would not have been in touch with Dennis Good's daughter Jennifer Tyrrell, who has done a fantastic job of liaising between me and her father.

One especially poignant email came from Marco Van Niekerk in South Africa, a good friend of Louis Vorster who was murdered aged just 46. It was evident from the way he wrote about Louis that he was a man of great integrity whose 'word was his bond'. How tragic that his life was cut short in such a violent way.

I had a memorable morning in the company of Charles Chatham's sons Richard and David, who were willing to share many anecdotes and photographs of their father. John Goodreds has told so much information about his father Bill, as did Ron Jones's son Ian. Cynthia Rudge was kind enough to speak to me about her husband Lloyd. Martin Lines, the grandson on John Spilsbury, helped fill in some gaps about his grandfather, who made his debut alongside his good friend Lloyd Rudge.

Ann Bennett was equally forthcoming in respect of the life of her father, Norman Bennett. I had no idea what a gifted rugby player he was. To my equal delight, there is a family connection to the much sought-after Bennett's Ice Cream, always to be found at the New Road ground in Worcester.

Alf Tasker's wife, Margaret and her son, Bradley, have been in touch from their home in Australia, Bradley is delighted that, as he told me, *'my father is being immortalised in the book, because he deserves it'*. That comment alone captures the sentiment behind producing this work.

In another poignant reminder that cricket is a game filled with nostalgia and happy memories, Lynda Collins, daughter of Harry

Moule, enjoyed recalling with fondness the life of her father. To the end, cricket played a massive part in Harry's life and she said that '*his funeral was cricket-themed and he went off the pitch wearing his Worcester tie*'. He was one of the 52 never to be forgotten and a Worcestershire man to the end.

# Introduction

Before putting pen to paper, my first task was to determine the complete list of players who were to feature; however, my first dilemma soon arose which begged the question of whether or not Nick Compton met my criteria. After all, he had played, as a 'guest', for Worcestershire in a first-class fixture against the Touring Australians at New Road in 2013. He was not, though, a member of the Club's playing staff, so I decided that he should not be included in the full list.

Instead, I decided to acknowledge his contribution in this introduction and asked his captain on the day, Daryl Mitchell, to comment on his selection for the game.

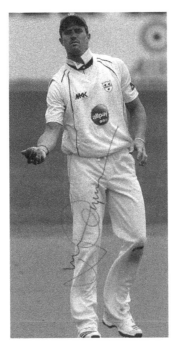

*Nick Compton in action during the match against Australia.*

Daryl Mitchell:

> 'It came about at the request of the ECB [England and Wales Cricket Board], or more specifically Andy Flower. Nick had been in and around the England Test team and was in the thoughts of the selectors for the first Ashes Test. From memory, we were in the middle of the domestic T-20 competition so at that point there wasn't much first-class cricket happening.

> 'We were asked if we could accommodate Nick. Bumpy [Steve Rhodes, the coach] discussed it with me and we were more than happy to oblige for three reasons:

> 1. It would strengthen us against international opposition.
> 2. What a great opportunity it would be for our young batters to learn from an international player.
> 3. It was felt that if there was anything we could do to help England versus the 'old enemy' then we should do it.

> 'Nick was great in and around the changing room. He's a thoroughly nice bloke and fitted in very well for that whole week. In line with the second point above, Bumpy facilitated an informal question-and-answer session one evening, which not only benefited him but gave the batters the opportunity to pick Nick's brains.

> 'He shared his thoughts on batting and his rise to Test cricket. Two things stood out to me. One was that he identified a void in English cricket that he could fill, as someone who was prepared to bat for hours on end and occupy the crease for as long as possible while the stroke makers could play around him.

> 'The other point was how he went about it and took himself to some really "dark places" in training (literally at times), facing a 90-mph machine in a poorly lit sports hall and

*working purely on survival. He took the old adage "train hard, play easy" to the very extreme.'*

Compton top-scored in Worcestershire's first innings with 79 and followed it with 26 in the second innings, but did not play Test cricket again until the Boxing Day Test at Durban in 2015.

My second dilemma concerned the players who had made their debuts in 1919, the first time that first-class cricket had been played since World War One. Surely the matches they played against other counties would constitute the awarding of their colours? The answer was found in Andrew Thomas's outstanding book *Pears 150 – The life and times of Worcestershire County Cricket Club 1865 – 2014* as to reason why not.

*'Due to the perilous financial situation after The War, Club Chairman, Judge Amphlett, reported that when the Dean and Chapter had thought the Club would fold, they had contemplated taking away the lease from the Club and letting it to 'a public body in Worcester'. Hearing that the Club was anxious to continue The Dean said the new five-year lease would be at an increased rent. The committee accepted unanimously, Major Bill Taylor's suggestion for an amateur team with one or two professionals, playing friendly two-day county matches and social games and not to re-join the County Championship in 1919.'*

In addition, following the Advisory County Cricket Committee meeting at Lord's, it was reported that: *'Worcestershire had failed to qualify for the Championship because it had been too late to obtain the necessary minimum of 12 fixtures. Subsequently it embarked on nine, friendly two-day matches which were afforded first-class status.'*

My final consideration was to decide whether to include career statistics for anyone who had also played for another county. Bearing in mind that this publication is dedicated purely to their time with Worcestershire, I decided against. In this day and age, with statistics readily available, it is straightforward to check these through other sources.

It has been rewarding to undertake the research, which has resulted in uncovering some outstanding stories of bravery, academic expertise and successful careers away from the cricket field, although some are tinged with sadness because of lives lost too soon. I have had the help of friends Sean Cullen and Sandra Taylor, both of whom have provided expert help and guidance in terms of the military careers of some of the players.

Worcestershire CCC life member and good friend Clive O'Donnell has provided outstanding help, support and feedback. He has undertaken some remarkable and diligent research to complement my work, and has the happy 'knack' of finding rare and unusual sources of information. Above all else, we have been able to find at least one photograph of each player, something which has been absent for too long.

I have also been lucky enough to establish contact with 16 of the 17 surviving players and their first-hand recollections have provided probably *the* most valuable of resources. It has been a privilege to speak with them.

My thanks also go to the help from the countless family members of those players no longer alive; they have provided a wealth of unique anecdotes which I have re-told. Special thanks go to John Chadd, who for so many years has championed both Herefordshire and Worcestershire cricket, for writing the foreword. In doing so, he said it was wonderful to re-live so many happy memories, all of which came flooding back.

It would be inappropriate for me to identify one favourite profile from the 52, but establishing contact with Dennis Good in Canada is something I shall treasure. I had been trying to contact Dennis for many years and had been thwarted at each step of the way until now.

Aged 94 (and Worcestershire's oldest surviving first-class cricketer) he is not in good health; however, his family has enjoyed helping him remember his cricketing days with fondness. They have been very helpful in relaying messages from him. That alone has made this the most worthwhile exercise alongside celebrating the achievements of the 52 – Worcestershire's Forgotten First-Class Cricketers. I hope you enjoy reading all about them.

# BARLEY

## JACK CHARLES BARLEY – RIGHT-HAND BAT, WICKET-KEEPER

Born: Eton, Buckinghamshire, 4 December 1887
Died: Surfers Paradise, Queensland, Australia, 26 October 1956

*Jack Barley 1930s portrait.*

First-class matches for Worcestershire: 1 versus Oxford University, The Parks, Oxford, 17, 18, 19 June 1909

Innings: 2; Not out: 1; Runs: 1; Highest score: 1; Caught: 1; Stumped: 1; Did not bowl

*In a 12-a-side game, Oxford University won by 42 runs. Thomas Sheppard was also making his debut for Worcestershire in this game and Guy Pawson represented Oxford University. Both players feature elsewhere in this publication. The University was indebted to Charles Hooman, who scored 102 in their second innings. Barley's moment of glory came when he combined with Worcestershire's legendary 'lob bowler' George Simpson-Hayward to dismiss Oxford's Frederick Turner (himself a Scottish rugby union international), who was stumped for a single. Thomas Sheppard was also making his debut for Worcestershire in this game and appears elsewhere in this publication.*

Within a week of making his debut for Worcestershire against Oxford University, Tonbridge School-educated Barley made his only appearance *for* the University in an innings and 98-run victory against Surrey. Three University batsmen were to score a hundred in the first innings. This was, however, the last of his four first-class matches; he had previously appeared for Sussex in 1908 and Leveson-Gower's XI in 1909. While he did not receive his Blue at Oxford, he represented the Authentics and was awarded the much-coveted Harlequins cap.

Studying at St John's College Oxford, he gained a second-class degree in Modern History in 1911 and an MA in 1912. The University's *Bystander Magazine* of August 1909 shows that he took an active part in the archery club. Interestingly, the caption in the magazine states that: '*The only archery club in either university: it meets only in the summer, on Thursdays, and devotes a deal of its energies to entertaining the fair sex.*'

*St John's College Oxford, archery club, 1909.*

On leaving university, Barley worked for the Civil Service as a cadet for the British Solomon Islands protectorate from 1912–1914. During the War he was a sapper – second class – with the Royal Engineers Transport Corps, thereafter becoming first district officer British Solomon Islands acting resident for 1917, 1921, 1929 and 1932.

He was also appointed as district officer and commissioner for the Western Pacific from 1915–1923 and 1924–25 and was seconded for duty as district commissioner for Fiji from 1925–1933.

*Picnic at Gela, approximately, 1910.*

In May 1933, Barley married Florence Doughty from Queensland and spent time in Sydney before setting sail on RMS *Niagara* for his new appointment as resident commissioner Gilbert and Ellice Islands, a post he held from 1934 until his retirement in 1941, when the Japanese took control of the colony.

One point of interest; when Amelia Earhart, the American aviation pioneer, 'disappeared' over the central Pacific on July 2 1937, Barley was part of the unsuccessful search party in the ship RCS (Royal Colony Ship) *Nimanoa*, a two-masted ketch assigned to the colonial administration in the Gilbert and Ellice Islands.

On retirement, Jack Barley farmed in Queensland until his death.

# BARRETT

## BRIAN JOSEPH BARRETT – RIGHT-HAND BAT, RIGHT-ARM MEDIUM FAST

Born: Pakuranga, Auckland, New Zealand, 16 November 1966

*Brian Barrett and his wife Galina.*

First-class matches for Worcestershire: 1 versus Cambridge University, Fenner's, Cambridge, 12, 13, 14 June 1985.

Innings: Did not bat; Caught: 0; Wickets: 1; Best bowling: 1-40

*Match drawn. While Worcestershire entertained Zimbabwe at New Road, seven players were given first-class debuts in the match at Cambridge. Three of them – Lawrence Smith, Stuart Lampitt and Paul Bent – all subsequently played Championship cricket. The other four – Brian Barrett, along with Harshad Patel, Mel Hussain and Mike Scothern who feature elsewhere in this publication – were not afforded the same opportunity.*

*Thanks to half-centuries from acting captain and wicket-keeper, David Humphries (62 not out) and David Banks (50 not out), a crisis was averted and Worcestershire posted 216-5 declared. Bad weather restricted the University's reply to 143-6 with Barrett claiming the wicket of Shaun Gorman for 0.*

Educated at Edgewater College in Auckland, Barrett progressed to club cricket in the city. It was here he was spotted by Worcestershire fast bowler Paul Pridgeon, who helped create the opportunity for him to play in England. His introduction to cricket in the UK was with Dudley in the Birmingham League, a side managed by former Worcestershire player Jack Sedgley.

Barrett recalls his first visit to New Road in 1985: '*It was a brisk morning and after a quick briefing from Paul Pridgeon in the car I joined the squad for an outdoor net session. Adjusting to the change in temperature and trying to roll my arm over with three layers of jumpers was a challenge in itself. I just wanted to bowl fast.*'

Following a return of nine wickets from six second XI games, Worcestershire Secretary Mike Vockins approached Barrett regarding his eligibility to play as a 'local' player. Barrett recalls: '*When my Irish-born dad was mentioned, Mike commented that Kevin Curran was playing as a 'local' for Gloucestershire because of his Irish mum or dad. Application forms were sent to the TCCB followed by various discussions and interviews, with Mike and the committee doing a lot of work on my behalf. On 10 August 1985 I was offered an engagement with the County as a local player for the rest of the season and for 1986.*'

The game at Cambridge held happy memories for Barrett and once more he recalls the events: '*To be playing in such a place at a university so rich and deep in history was quite surreal. My Kiwi slander was wasted on the educated Cambridge batsmen, but it was enjoyed by my team-mates, especially Humpty (David Humphries) behind the stumps.*

'*One other memory of this game was the number of bikes everywhere. I'd never owned a bike, so after a night out at the end of day two I decided to return early to the hotel. I couldn't resist the opportunity to ride one of these bikes, and carefully selected a sparkling blue one with a basket and a bell. A most enjoyable ride was undertaken, the bike was parked neatly at the hotel and the owner found the next day.*

*'I returned in 1986, after an extremely busy New Zealand season, playing first-class cricket and youth internationals against Australia. My contract was signed and my salary was £3,400 for the season. I would have played for free.'*

*Worcestershire CCC 1986 – Brian Barrett, back row, sixth from the left.*

Barrett's second season playing for Worcestershire seconds and Kidderminster in the Birmingham League was interrupted when he was selected for the New Zealand tour of England later that summer. The decision now was to determine whether the future lay with club or country. He explains: '*I chose country, which was an easy decision at the time but in hindsight the wrong one from a career perspective. I was only 19 and the County – mainly Mike Vockins and my mentor Pridge (Paul Pridgeon) – had done so much for me; I should have considered better advice. Because of this I lost my eligibility to play as a local and, sadly, I never returned to New Road again.*'

Barrett continued to play first-class cricket back in New Zealand for Northern Districts in the Shell Trophy but a lack of form and neglected injuries from being over-bowled as a young fast bowler took its toll. Aged just 23 he retired, and after a few seasons playing and coaching in Auckland embarked on a career outside cricket.

Fortunately he had completed a bachelor of business studies and began his first job with a company as an assistant groundsman. Cleaning the toilets and changing rooms were part of the job initially; however, Barrett worked his way up to contract manager, managing more than 80 staff.

He then joined one of New Zealand's biggest companies, Fletcher Building, and was one of the senior managers in their concrete division for a few years. At this time Barrett's wife Galina gave birth to twin girls, which prompted him to leave the corporate world and buy a real estate and property management company, an environment he has enjoyed working in for the past 16 years.

The girls have graduated from university and have embarked on their own professional careers. Barrett now enjoys an active lifestyle and watching a multitude of sports from the sidelines.

# BENNETT

## NORMAN OSBORN BENNETT – RIGHT-HAND BAT, RIGHT-ARM MEDIUM

Born: Putney, London, 21 September 1922
Died: Dinckley, near Blackburn, Lancashire, 7 July 2005

*Norman Bennett representing England at rugby union.*

First-class matches for Worcestershire: 1 versus Combined Services, New Road, Worcester, 31 July 1, 2 August 1946

Innings: 2; Not out: 0; Runs: 10; Highest score: 8; Caught: 1; Did not bowl

*Combined Services won by five wickets. Thanks to 107 by Don Kenyon and half-centuries from Mike Ainsworth (50 not out) and Reg Perks (51) – all of whom, ironically, played for Worcestershire – the visitors closed on 429 all out. Norman Bennett's catch helped in the dismissal of Reg Perks off the bowling of Roly Jenkins.*

*Dismissed for 232, Worcestershire were 'held together', with half-centuries from Allan White (58) and Roly Jenkins (69 not out), Bennett's contribution being two. Following on, Worcestershire were dismissed for 280, White top-scoring with 95. Set 84 to win, the Combined Services reached their target for the loss of five wickets.*

*John Collinson and Dennis Good were also making their debuts for Worcestershire in this game and feature elsewhere in this publication.*

For many years the record books were incorrect by showing the name 'M Bennett'. It was not until 1999 when I spoke to him that this was corrected.

Bennett (also known as 'Nobby' in cricketing circles and 'Billy' in rugby circles), was educated at Epsom College and lived in London where his father – also called Norman – ran a large milk delivery round and his grandfather, Robert, ran the dairy. Some years later the family moved to Worcester where, today, they still farm. They are well known for the production of Bennett's Ice Cream.

Bennett's aunt was married to Fred Hunt, the legendary groundsman at New Road, Worcester, who was the man responsible for creating and establishing the playing surface that we know today.

While studying at St Mary's Medical School in Paddington (as in later years did the great Welsh rugby union full back, J.P.R. Williams) Bennett 's prowess as a rugby player blossomed.

Towards the end of the War, Bennett joined the Royal Navy based in Portsmouth and, because he enlisted, certain medical protocols were relaxed and his time counted towards his practical assessments. The Navy list for October 1948, shows him as Norman Osborn Bennett MRCS, LRCP and temporary surgeon lieutenant.

Representing Harlequins, Waterloo and Combined Services at rugby union, greater honours were to follow when he made his international debut for England against Wales (playing at centre) on 18 January 1947 in Cardiff. Also making his debut in that game was Micky Steele-Bodger who had a 73-year association with and later became president of the world-famous Barbarians Invitation XV.

In the book *Behind the Rose – Playing for England* the game at The Arms Park is described: *'The team obviously was much changed. For the first match in Cardiff, only Dickie Guest spanned the years since international rugby had ceased. Among England's 14 new caps were Norman 'Nim' Hall, Keith Scott and Norman Bennett who formed a midfield entirely drawn from St Mary's Hospital.*

*'Hall, Scott and Bennett were medical students and the brains behind the successful St Mary's side that had dominated other students and servicemen stationed in England in wartime club games. Their Club's finest hour was in January 1945 when they ended Coventry's incredible run of 72 successive wins stretching back to December 1941 with an 8-3 win at Teddington Hall.'*

*England v Scotland, Twickenham, 15 March 1947. England 25, Scotland 5. Bennett is standing second from the left.*

After marrying Rosalie Graham, Bennett joined his father-in-law's medical practice in Wigan as a GP, where he remained throughout his working career, living in the Ribble Valley and commuting to his place of work.

A great man for ideas, Bennett bred rabbits commercially, had a herd of Murray Grey cows and set up the Owls Restaurant in Wigan.

Still keen on his cricket, he was involved with the Forty Club, for whom he played from 1943–1980, was a member of MCC and played for Cheshire Gents, Cross Arrows and the great 'wandering' club Free Foresters. Playing for the Buccaneers against the British Empire XI at Lord's in 1942, he top-scored with 62 not out in a side containing the Surrey trio of the Bedser twins and Laurie Fishlock.

# BRINTON

## PERCIVAL ROBERT BRINTON – RIGHT-HAND BAT

Born: Moor Hall, Lower Mitton, near Kidderminster, Worcestershire,
5 February 1873
Died: Oxford, 14 May 1958

*Balliol College, Oxford,1891–92. Percival Brinton*
*(back row, extreme right). Seated in the middle is Malcolm Jardine,*
*father of Douglas Jardine.*

First-class matches for Worcestershire: 1 versus Oxford University,
The Parks, Oxford, 13, 14, 15 June 1904

Innings: 1; Not out: 0; Runs: 1; Highest score: 1; Caught: 0; Did
not bowl

*Worcestershire won by an innings and 93 runs. In the University's*
*first innings of 172, George Wilson claimed 9-75 and in reply*

*Worcestershire amassed 467, thanks to 118 from H.K. Foster and half-centuries from Fred Bowley (55), William Burns (69) and wicket-keeper Fred Wheldon (68). Batting at number eight, Brinton was dismissed for a single by Adolph von Ernsthausen.*

*Oxford were bowled out for 202 in their second innings, John Cuffe claiming 5-58, only Kenneth Carlisle with 56 putting up any resistance.*

The son of John Brinton – chairman of the world-renowned Brinton's Carpets and MP for Kidderminster – Percival Brinton was educated at Winchester College before studying classics at Balliol College, Oxford between 1891 and 1895. There he played football and represented the College at cricket, before graduating with a second-class BA in literae humaniores. During the university holidays he enjoyed Worcestershire life, riding with the Berkeley Hunt. An MA followed in 1904.

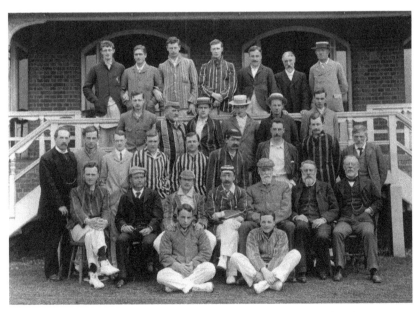

*Balliol College 'past and present' 1904 – Brinton is on the front row, extreme left, seated.*

Between 1904 and 1908 (during which time Brinton became a doctor of divinity from Cuddesdon Theological College, Oxford, in 1905) he was curate at St Mary's, Portsea and then domestic chaplain to the Bishop of Bombay between 1908 and 1910. He was then appointed chaplain of All Saints' Church, Malabar Hill, Bombay, a post he held between 1910 and 1911, returning thereafter to England.

One of the society weddings of the year in 1912 saw Brinton's sister Martha (known as Patty) marry the Reverend Geoffrey Gordon with the service being performed by Percival. An impressive guest list included Princess Christian Schleswig-Holstein, third daughter of Queen Victoria.

In 1916 Brinton married Florence Heston Baddeley and on 6 September 1917 their daughter Mary was born. During World War One, Percival served in the Church Army.

By 1920, the electoral roll shows the family living in Colchester, where Brinton was Rector of All Saints' Church, and by 1929 he was Rector of Hambledon, a fitting parish for a cricketer. In the same year, playing for the clergy in the annual charity match against the Buckinghamshire police in Slough, he scored 105 out of a total of 192-5 declared. The Reverend J. Denning of Hungerford, who was in his 70s, took five cheap police wickets by bowling wily underarm lobs akin to the great Worcestershire lob bowler George Simpson-Hayward. The newspaper headline 'Aged cleric's cricket skill' captured the moment.

A prolific writer, by 1934 Brinton had translated Lewis Carroll's *The Hunting of the Snark* and *Gray's Elegy* into Latin and had several other works published, including a *Memoir of Edwin James Palmer, seventh Bishop of Bombay* 1908-1929: A memoir. In 1936, having reached the ripe old age of 63, he still found time to play for the victorious clergy side in the annual fixture against Buckinghamshire police, scoring 11 runs on this occasion.

During the 1940s Brinton worked as Rector of Holy Trinity Church in Darlington and latterly moved to Oxford where he died at the John Radcliffe Hospital. He left an estate of £29, 118 10s 2d.

His brother Reginald, a future chairman of Brinton's, played 13 matches for Worcestershire as an amateur between 1903 and 1909.

# BROWN

## ALAN BROWN – RIGHT-HAND BAT, WICKET-KEEPER

Born: Darwen, Lancashire, 23 December 1957

*Portrait of Alan Brown in 2020.*

First-class matches for Worcestershire: 1 versus Oxford University, The Parks, Oxford, 16, 18, 19 June 1979

Innings: Did not bat; Caught: 2; Stumped: 0; Did not bowl

*Match drawn. Worcestershire declared on 311-5 thanks to half-centuries from Phil Neale (65), Dipak Patel (64) and Basil D'Oliveira (51). Greg Watson with 3-56 helped dismiss the students for 179 and in their second innings Worcestershire declared on 147-2 with Alan Ormrod scoring 56.*

*Requiring 280 to win, Oxford closed on 259-8 thanks to 82 from John Claughton and 56 from Jonathan Orders. On one of the rare occasions that he bowled, Younis Ahmed claimed 3-33 from his 14 overs.*

Brown's first trial game for Worcestershire was a two-day match against Glamorgan at The Gnoll, Neath on 19 and 20 July 1976. He had previously played for Lancashire under-18s but was regarded as the second-wicket wicket-keeper behind Chris Scott who was younger and considered a better wicket-keeper.

Brown recalls vividly the game: '*Worcestershire had lost the Benson and Hedges Cup Final on the Saturday. Basil D'Oliveira got injured and batted heroically on one leg and I had watched Cedric Boyns bowl instead of him and then I was playing cricket with Cedric on the Monday!*

'*I was nervous and excited because immediately after this match there was a second two-day game against Gloucestershire at The Recreational Trust Ground at Lydney.*

'*The first piece of excitement was that we travelled on a really posh coach, the sort of coach people look at and wonder which stars are on board. We also stopped in what I thought were really top-of-the-range hotels. I don't want to overplay it, but I am the youngest of seven and my hometown, Darwen, is a traditional northern working-class industrial town. I had never been on a posh coach and a caravan in Cleveleys was the best accommodation I had been in.*'

In addition to appearances for Worcestershire's Club and Ground XI, between 1976 and 1979 Brown played a total of 33 second XI matches for Worcestershire. Pictured here (in the doorway) he is taking the field for the seconds in the game against Derbyshire at Evesham Sports Club Ground on 7 and 8 August 1978. In reply to Derbyshire's 231, Worcestershire were dismissed for 64 and 96, losing by an innings and 71 runs.

*Versus Derbyshire Second XI, Evesham Sports Ground 1978. Brown is standing in the doorway.*

Brown's first-half-century came in the drawn game against Northamptonshire seconds at Denton Road, Horton in August 1978, with 53 out of a total of 154-8 declared. Two catches and a second-innings 26 not out rounded off a sound performance.

One of the outstanding highlights of his time playing second XI cricket was having the pleasure to bat with one of the greats, Tom Graveney:

*'He came to captain the seconds for one game against Somerset at Bridgwater in early July and we had partnerships of 40 and 26 in the game. Somerset had a very fast bowler, David Gurr, who had me hopping about as I did my best to keep him out. Batting at number 11, Tom, on the other hand, looked as though he had all the time in the world. It made me realise I was a very ordinary batsman but I was thrilled when he commented that he was pleased with my application; praise indeed.'*

Brown described the second highlight of his career as having the opportunity to bat with Basil D'Oliveira. This happened in the game at New Road in the draw against Gloucestershire seconds from the 27 to 29 June in 1979. Two strong sides featured, Worcestershire including Martin Weston, Tim Curtis, Cedric Boyns, Steve Henderson and Paul Pridgeon, while the visitors featured Chris Broad, David Shepherd, Phil Bainbridge, Mike Garnham and David Graveney.

Talking about the game Brown says: *'I was in awe of Basil. Having left Darwen Grammar School I was at college and the late-70s was part of my political awakening; anti-Apartheid was big news.*

*'I was aware and fascinated by Basil's story and his shocking omission – initially – from the MCC tour to South Africa in 1968–69. Then the awful South African regime refused to allow him to tour. I remember Basil's dignity throughout all of this ... and there I was playing in the same team as him. He was near the end of his career so was playing a lot of second XI cricket; however, he was always lovely to me.'*

At Dale Field, Collingham, Brown struck his second half-century in the drawn game against Nottinghamshire second XI. A score of 173 from Steve Henderson, 91 from James Robson and 57 from Alan, allowed Worcestershire to declare on 407-8.

One element of Brown's days at New Road which he remembers well were the changing facilities in the old pavilion. He told me: *'The senior professionals were downstairs and the younger players upstairs. During my time, Phil Neale graduated downstairs but I have many happy memories and had lots of laughs upstairs with Paul Pridgeon, Dipak Patel, Barry Jones and Steve Henderson.'*

Brown had made his senior debut in the John Player Sunday League game at Lord's on 17 June 1979, the 'rest day' of the Oxford University fixture. He recalls that his preparation was not ideal: *'I was not expecting to play so my kit was still in Oxford, but a neck injury to David Humphries, just 30 minutes before the start of play, meant I was needed and had to play in borrowed kit. To make things worse I'd just eaten an enormous Sunday dinner!'*

At the end of 1979, however, Brown was released: *'Obviously it was disappointing, but deep down I knew I wasn't good enough. I really gave it my best shot, trained hard and tried hard.*

*'You found out if you were retained by letter. It would have been better if someone had had a face-to-face conversation, but perhaps that's how it was in those days. I rented a room in Cedric's [Cedric Boyns] house that year and he was also released; his was a much more contentious decision. It was a sad time, but people were really nice and ultimately I had played cricket at a level I hadn't really dreamed of and took away some great memories.'*

In 2005, during a meeting in the chief executive's office at New Road I came across Brown's John Player League third place medal from 1979. Returning it to him I received a letter by return. With his customary good humour, he explained: *Having been released – sacked as my children Andrew and Katy call it – I wasn't aware I was entitled to a medal. I recall, though, receiving a cheque for £8.52, an 11th of a 16th of £1,500 for finishing third.'*

Returning to mainstream work, Brown, who had completed a bachelor of education degree at St John's College in York, trained as a PE teacher and taught for 38 years. He had completed his degree during his time at Worcester and had toured the Caribbean with the British Colleges in a squad that included Chris Broad.

He enjoyed teaching very much and for the final 10 years of his career was deputy head at a special school for pupils with behaviour issues, which he describes as a challenging and rewarding time. He retired in 2016.

In retirement Brown plays golf (very badly is his description of his game, but I'm sure he's being modest) and he and his wife of

38 years, Margaret, walk a dog for the Cinnamon Trust Charity twice a week. A lifelong supporter, he still follows the fortunes of his favourite football team, Blackburn Rovers.

*Worcestershire Club and Ground XI, 1978.*
*Brown is on the back row, extreme left.*

# BROWNELL

## ERIC LINDSAY DOUGLAS BROWNELL – RIGHT-HAND BAT

Born: Hobart, Tasmania, Australia, 7 November 1876
Died: Windsor, New South Wales, Australia, 22 October 1945

*Eric Brownell of the First Imperial Tasmanian Bushmen.*

First-class matches for Worcestershire: 1 versus Oxford University, The Parks, Oxford, 11, 12, 13 June 1908

Innings: 2; Not out: 0; Runs: 28; Highest score: 21; Caught: 1; Did not bowl

*Worcestershire won by 332 runs. In the first innings they were indebted to George Simpson-Hayward who, out of a total of 185, scored 105 in just 80 minutes.*

*Simpson-Hayward continued his excellent form and took 6-13 in the University's first innings of 85. Batting for a second time, Worcestershire scored 362, William Burns striking 146 (in just over two hours at the crease). Leaving Oxford 463 to win, all-rounder Ted Arnold made light work of their second innings claiming 7-51 as Oxford were dismissed for 130.*

*Eric Brownell contributed 21 in Worcestershire's first innings and seven runs in the second innings where he became one of Humphrey Gilbert's six victims. Gilbert finished with match figures of 11-224 and went on to play 72 matches for Worcestershire between 1921 and 1930.*

*Guy Pawson, John Winnington and Freddy Grisewood were also making their debuts for Worcestershire in this game and feature elsewhere in this publication.*

Eric Brownell was a well-travelled career soldier. With the First Tasmanian Imperial Bushmen he set sail from Tasmania on 26 April 1900 to fight in the Boer War, returning home on 5 August 1901.

In 1901 Trooper Brownell was mentioned in Lord Kitchener's Despatch but it was not until 2 October that news of his bravery filtered through in the *London Evening Standard*. It is reproduced here as it was written and reads:

'*8 July 1901 – Tasmanian Imperial Bushmen: Trooper E L D Brownell (promoted Corporal), on May 9 at Ganna Hock, Cape Colony, showed distinguished bravery in fighting with only one man (Private J E Wharbeston, same corps) 20 Boers, killing 2 Boers and 2 horses; finding he could not escape, and his comrade being mortally wounded, shot both horses to prevent them falling into the enemy's hands; taken prisoner and stripped; he was released, when he walked into camp and at once took an ambulance, remained out all night, and brought in Private Wharbeston.*'

Eric Brownell was shot in the shoulder during this incident and on a separate occasion refers to further action he saw, this being detailed in his War diary. He comments on the awful conditions he encounters, the sights he sees, all of which left an indelible impact on him:

'*On seeing our column safely over the ridge, the Boers made off in a northerly direction, making their retreat safe by setting the veldt on fire. There was a strong wind blowing at the time and the flames spread so rapidly through the long grass that we had some difficulty in saving part of our transport.*

'*As it was, one ambulance waggon had to be outspanned and left to the mercy of the flames. In lending a hand with the*

23

*waggons, I was soon left behind by our column, and when going off at a full gallop to regain my former position, the horse trod in a rabbit burrow, fell heavily and rolled on top of me. However, I was on again in an instant, but got a severe shaking.'*

Army records state that: *He made no further comment in his diary yet these notes were written in the Field Hospital, Johannesburg, where Trooper Brownell is lying with both knees crushed, the result of his horse falling with, and on him; otherwise he is in excellent health and spirits.*

He was invalided back to Tasmania where news arrived of his commission – for meritorious conduct in South Africa under Colonel Watchorn – in the Worcestershire Regiment which was stationed in Tipperary, Ireland.

Second Lieutenant Brownell found time to play cricket during his time in Ireland. In August 1903 the 3rd Battalion played Clonmel and won by 43 runs thanks to 60 from Lieutenant Nesbitt. Arnold Nesbitt was to play one game for Worcestershire against Middlesex at Lord's in 1914 but sadly lost his life fighting at Ploegsteert Wood in the November of the same year. Brownell finished second in the regiment's batting averages, scoring 260 runs at an average of 26.00.

In December 1905, Brownell played for The Europeans against Madras Presidency at Madras Cricket Club. In an innings and 147-run defeat he acquitted himself well by scoring 46 and, opening the bowling, taking 3-112.

Greater success followed in July 1908 when he represented the Gentlemen of Worcestershire versus the Gentlemen of Herefordshire in a two-day game at New Road, Worcester. He scored 186 out of 461 in an innings and 198-run victory. The side included three Worcestershire players, Arthur Isaac, Bill Taylor and William Burns.

On June 30, 1909, Brownell married Ilene Stenhouse-Clarke in a ceremony at Paddington in Middlesex. Her father was a retired colonel, the First Worcestershire Regiment. In August despite losing by an innings and 96 runs, he scored 124 not out for the Gentlemen of Worcestershire against the Gentlemen of Warwickshire.

*2nd Battalion Worcestershire Regiment Officers*
*(Jhansi, India – December 1911). Brownell is seated on the left.*

A posting to India followed and by 1912 Brownell had been promoted to colonel, 3rd Battalion, Worcestershire Regiment. In 1914 he fought at Mons and sustained a gunshot wound to the shoulder and was admitted on 28 October to Queen Alexandra's Hospital, Millbank in London to recuperate. He was discharged on 23 November.

*Portrait of Colonel Eric Brownell.*

Colonel Brownell was then seconded to the Royal Military College of Australia, based in Duntroon in Canberra. Their journal states that: '*A special bombing school has been formed under the guidance of Captain Brownell as part of his role as an instructor on tactics.*'

By the time War had ended, he had been promoted to the rank of major, having been awarded the British War Medal, the 1914 Star with clasp and the Allied Victory Medal. He settled in Windsor, New South Wales where he became an orchardist; however, he continued his travels, shipping documents showing that he made trips to Buenos Aires, Gibraltar, Bombay and New York.

# BURR

### FREDERICK BONHAM BURR – RIGHT-HAND BAT

Born: Blacklands, Hastings, Sussex, 2 August 1887
Died: (in action) Kemmel, West Flanders, Belgium, 12 March 1915

*Portrait of Frederick Burr.*

First-class matches for Worcestershire: 1 versus Oxford University, The Parks, Oxford, 25, 26, 27 May 1911

Innings: 2; Not out: 1; Runs: 46; Highest score: 39; Caught: 1; Did not bowl

*Worcestershire won by six wickets. Oxford were dismissed for 313 with Burr taking the catch to dismiss Ronald Lagden, an English rugby union international. Worcestershire replied with 359 and were indebted to George Simpson-Hayward for his 130, scored in precisely two hours, an innings which contained 17 fours and two sixes. Batting at number four, Burr acquitted himself well in scoring 39 before he was dismissed by John Vidler.*

*Thanks to a second four-wicket haul from Bill Taylor (4-88 and 4-40) plus Ted Arnold with 3-29, the students were dismissed for just 140. Finishing on 95-4 with Arnold 63 not out, Worcestershire got home comfortably.*

*Major Davis and Guy Davidge were also making their debuts for Worcestershire in this game and feature elsewhere in this publication.*

The son of Reverend George and Caroline Burr, Frederick lived at Highfields Park in Halesowen. The family had owned the Hayseech Gun Barrel works in Rowley Regis, West Midlands for many years.

John Burr senior, a Warwickshire man, moved to Halesowen in 1775, beginning his career as a millwright. In 1801 John built the works at Hayseech and a stone in the gable of the grinding shop at the entrance to the works inscribed 'Burr 1801' is still in evidence today, the building being used as the Industrial Gun Barrel Centre.

Educated at Sandroyd and then Denstone College between 1900 and 1907, Burr was awarded his cricket colours in 1902 and was captain in 1907. He gained his rugby colours in 1905 and 1906 and was also captain of fives in 1906.

He 'went up' to Keble College, Oxford, in the Michaelmas term of 1907 and was a member of the Authentics Cricket Club. He participated in the freshmen's cricket trial in 1908 and was a member of the cricket first XI from 1908–1911, taking on the captaincy in 1910. He had a seniors' cricket trial in 1909 and on occasion played for the Gentlemen of Worcestershire. He won his oar in The Torpids, 1910–1911 and also played water polo.

In a friendly fixture, Burr played once more for Worcestershire against Staffordshire at the County Ground, Stoke in 1910. He was one of four victims for John Nichols, who played five matches for Worcestershire between 1902 and 1904. In August of the same year, a score of 78 in the second innings of the second XI game for Worcestershire against Warwickshire seconds added a degree of respectability in the innings and 119-run defeat.

A member of the Authors' Club, he wrote several poems under the title of 'The Strummings of a Lyre' published in 1912 and completed a bachelor of arts in 1913 and a master of arts in

1914. Although he was studying for the Church at Cuddesdon Theological College, he did not complete his studies due to the outbreak of war.

His military connections were forged when he played cricket for the Reserve of Officers, Worcestershire Officer Training Corps, in 1913. Second Lieutenant Burr joined the 3rd Battalion Worcestershire Regiment on 5 August 1914 and disembarked in France on 23 September.

*Second Lieutenant Frederick Burr, 3rd Battalion, Worcestershire Regiment.*

In March 1915, the British attacked the German lines in Artois, Neuve Chapelle. The Worcesters put in a diversionary attack at Spanbroek Mill on the spur south of Ypres but paid a heavy price. Nine officers and 38 other ranks were killed including Second Lieutenant Burr who was just 28 years of age. Of small consolation, he was awarded the 1914 Star, the Victory Medal and the British War Medal but more tragedy was to strike when his brother Alfred, from the First Special Company of Royal Engineers, was also killed on 24 March 1918 aged just 27.

Frederick Burr was buried at Kemmel Chateau Cemetery and his name is commemorated on the Halesowen memorial at St John the Baptist Church and the Oxford University Roll of Honour, which states that he attained the role of captain before he was killed.

*Kemmel Chateau Cemetery headstone.*

# CARMICHAEL

### EVELYN GEORGE MASSEY CARMICHAEL (CARMICHAEL OF CARMICHAEL, 29TH CHIEF OF THE CLAN) RIGHT-HAND BAT, RIGHT-ARM MEDIUM

Born: Upper Wick, Worcester, 3 April 1871
Died: Berrington Hall, Shrewsbury, Shropshire, 14 July 1959

*Portrait of Evelyn Carmichael.*

First-class matches for Worcestershire: 1 versus Oxford University, The Parks, Oxford, 18, 19, 20 May 1903

Innings: 2; Not out: 0; Runs: 6; Highest score: 5; Caught: 1; Did not bowl

*Oxford University won by 59 runs. Albert Bird (5-57) and George Wilson (4-33) helped to dismiss the students for 178 in their first innings. The visitors' reply lasted just 38 overs as they were bowled out for 98 with William Evans (5-61) and George Martin (5-26) – of Martin's Bank fame – bowling unchanged. Carmichael was one of Martin's victims: batting at number seven he was bowled for five runs.*

*Ironically, both Martin and Evans played Championship cricket for Worcestershire, Evans having made his debut in 1901 against*

*Sussex and Martin making his debut against Somerset in the July of 1903.*

*Bird with 7-41 in Oxford's second innings helped to dismiss them for 103 which meant that Worcestershire were left to score 184 for victory; however, thanks to Martin once more (4-40) they were bowled out for just 124.*

The son of Lieutenant-Colonel George Carmichael, Evelyn Carmichael was educated at Harrow School. He enjoyed playing cricket from an early age, representing Worcester under-17s against Hereford under-17s at Leominster in 1885. He made an inauspicious start, being dismissed without score as Worcester were bowled out for just 16.

In July 1891, playing at the wonderful Boughton Park ground in St John's, Worcester, in a drawn game against the Worcester Regiment, he struck 126 not out for Worcestershire out of a total of 242-5.

Continuing to play most of his cricket during the annual Boughton Cricket Week fixtures, in August 1892 he struck 141 not out for Worcestershire Club and Ground in the drawn game against Malvern. The following August playing for the Club and Ground team once more, he achieved his best bowling figures, a return of 8-38 from 20 overs against High Green at Croome Park.

Having begun his studies at Oriel College, Oxford on 22 October 1890, Carmichael completed a bachelor of arts degree in 1894 (and a master of arts degree in 1898). During the summer of 1894, two of the opponents for the Worcestershire cricket week were to be Uppingham Rovers and Incogniti, but Incogniti withdrew at short notice. In order to maintain the week's programme, Carmichael – a member of the cricket week committee – got together a 'scratch' team to oppose the County's Club and Ground XI, a side containing Fred Bowley, Harry Foster and Tom

Straw. In spite of their presence, 'his team' was victorious by 24 runs in a low-scoring game.

### Worcestershire Cricket Week.

## WORCESTERSHIRE v. E. G. M. CARMICHAEL'S XI.,

### August 3rd & 4th, 1894.

#### MR. CARMICHAEL'S XI.

| | 1st INNINGS. | | 2nd INNINGS. | |
|---|---|---|---|---|
| 1 | Mr. E. G. Carmichael b Millward | 14 | c Foster b Reiss | 14 |
| 2 | Mr. H. V. Plum b Raynor | 3 | c Millward b Powys-Keck | 27 |
| 3 | Mr. W. W. Greenstock c Foley b Raynor | 11 | c Foley b Reiss | 4 |
| 4 | Burrows b Millward | 2 | c Millward b Powys-Keck | 8 |
| 5 | Mr. R. E. Lyon b Millward | 0 | run out | 0 |
| 6 | Mr. J. C. Harris b Millward | 14 | b Reiss | 22 |
| 7 | Mr. A. W. Isaac c Reiss b Millward | 24 | not out | 27 |
| 8 | Mr. H. W. Pike b Raynor | 0 | b Latham | 2 |
| 9 | Captain C. C. How b Raynor | 10 | lbw b Millward | 16 |
| 10 | Willoughby c Boucher b Millward | 9 | b Millward | 1 |
| 11 | Aldridge not out | 2 | st Straw b Millward | 0 |
| | Extras | 6 | Extras | 6 |
| | Total | 104 | Total | 137 |

#### WORCESTERSHIRE.

| | 1st INNINGS. | | 2nd INNINGS. | |
|---|---|---|---|---|
| 1 | Bowley b Willoughby | 2 | b Willoughby | 19 |
| 2 | Straw c Carmichael b Aldridge | 24 | c Harris b Willoughby | 12 |
| 3 | Mr. R. B. Reiss b Willoughby | 11 | b Willoughby | 8 |
| 4 | Mr. H. K. Foster c Greenstock b Burrows | 7 | c Carmichael b Willoughby | 0 |
| 5 | Mr. P. H. Latham b Aldridge | 0 | c Pike b Burrows | 0 |
| 6 | Millward b Willoughby | 22 | b Willoughby | 0 |
| 7 | Mr. J. J. Sweetman b Burrows | 0 | run out | 0 |
| 8 | Mr. R. Boucher c Greenstock b Willoughby | 0 | c and b Aldridge | 0 |
| 9 | Mr. H. Powys-Keck b Burrows | 5 | b Aldridge | 1 |
| 10 | Raynor not out | 2 | b Aldridge | 17 |
| 11 | Mr. P. H. Foley c Willoughby b Burrows | 5 | not out | 2 |
| | Extras | 7 | Extras | 8 |
| | Total | 152 | Total | 65 |

### Worcestershire Cricket Club.

The Cricket Week will take place on the County Ground, at Boughton, on Aug. 1st, 2nd, 3rd, and 4th, when the following Matches will be played

#### v. UPPINGHAM ROVERS.
#### v. CARMICHAEL'S XI.

#### PLAY TO COMMENCE AT 12 O'CLOCK.

**THIS TICKET ADMITS ONE PERSON ON ANY ONE DAY.**
TO BE SHOWN AT THE GATE AND RETAINED.

*Scorecard and match ticket from E.G.M. Carmichael's XI versus Worcestershire Club and Ground, 1894.*

In the same year, Carmichael was 'called to the bar' and admitted as barrister of law at the Inner Temple. He was instrumental, in 1904, in drafting the law relating to the telegraph, the telephone and submarine cable.

In August 1895 Carmichael was included in the Worcestershire side playing in the Minor Counties Championship, a precursor to the Club gaining first-class status in 1899. His one appearance in the competition was in the match against Durham, at Kidderminster, which Worcestershire won by 43 runs.

Carmichael's involvement during Boughton Cricket Week continued, and this picture from 1898 shows him standing on the extreme left of the back row. Six players in this picture represented Worcestershire County Cricket Club once it had attained first-class status.

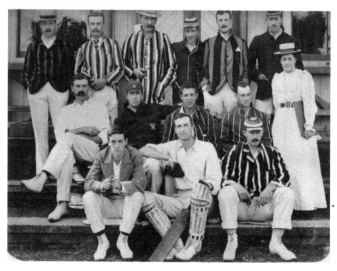

*Evelyn Carmichael (back row extreme left).*
*Boughton Cricket Week, 1898.*

In early 1903 Carmichael's father, Lieutenant-Colonel George Carmichael of the Derbyshire Regiment, who had fought in The Crimea, died. For his funeral in February the *County Advertiser for Staffordshire and Worcestershire* stated that: *'The streets were lined with large crowds who showed the deepest respect'*, with many dignitaries, including Stanley Baldwin, in attendance. The service was conducted by his old friend and Worcestershire cricketer, the Reverend E.E. Lea. He subsequently performed the marriage ceremony of Evelyn Carmichael's daughter some 37 years later in 1940.

On 14 and 15 August 1905 Carmichael represented MCC against Herefordshire at the Racecourse Ground in Hereford. He scored 89 in a second-wicket partnership of over a hundred, with his Worcestershire teammate, the legendary R.E. 'Tip' Foster. It was not enough to save them as Herefordshire won by eight wickets.

The following year he played for MCC once more in a game against Bourton Vale, Bourton-on-the-Water. On this occasion the Bourton side contained none other than the celebrated author, P.G. Wodehouse.

In a ceremony at St Paul's Church, Knightsbridge, on 29 February 1908, Carmichael married Dorothea Sutherland, the daughter of the late Sir James Colquhoun, Baronet of Colquhoun and Luss.

Following the birth of his daughter Georgina on 5 March 1909, Carmichael was pursuing ambitions in the political world. He was nominated as the Conservative Party candidate for North Monmouthshire and stood in the election early in 1910. Polling 4,335 votes, he was beaten by the Liberal candidate Reginald Mckenna, who polled 8,596 votes. In a long political career Mckenna served as First Lord of the Admiralty, home secretary and Chancellor of the Exchequer.

Carmichael's last cricket match was an appearance for Worcestershire second XI in a two-day game against Warwickshire second XI on 1 and 2 August 1910. In an innings and 119-run defeat the scorecard from the game tells its own story; however, Carmichael did take three of the eight Warwickshire wickets to fall.

*Scorecard from the game between Worcestershire Second XI and Warwickshire Second XI in 1910.*

His second daughter, Diana, was born on 8 July 1912. Carmichael's sense of public duty continued during World War One. In 1915 he was chairman of the Coventry Munitions Tribunal and military representative for the Colliery Courts for Shropshire, Herefordshire and Radnorshire in 1916. He was chairman of the House of Lords (pensions) Appeal Tribunal and was appointed an OBE in 1920.

In the same year, Carmichael was appointed chairman of the Walsall Court of Referees and held the office of justice of the peace (JP) for Staffordshire in 1923 and Shropshire in 1928. On 24 January 1924, a third daughter, Jean, was born. Carmichael went on to hold the position of 29th Chief of the Name and Arms of Carmichael from 12 August 1934.

In concluding his story, during the summer of 2020 I contacted Richard, the current chief of the Carmichael clan, who in an email, provided more detail as to the origins of the name:

'My connection is as a cousin and I've been 30th chief since 1981. My lines were chiefs of Carmichael and Anstruther, however, you cannot be chief of two clans/names in Scotland. As a result, a second senior branch claimed Carmichael from 1807 at the death of the 6th Earl of Hyndford until Evelyn's death in 1959. I addressed this by reuniting the land with the chiefship and abandoning the Anstruther chiefship claim in 1981.

'Evelyn's eldest daughter, Georgina Hermione Mary (Colville), and her only child, Sara Elizabeth (Colville), both agreed when my wife and I went to meet them on the south coast that year. I then presented the petition to the Lord Lyon King of Arms stating that it was a full 22 years after Evelyn's death and I was the entitled heir to the original lands at Carmichael.'

# CHADD

## JOHN ETHERIDGE CHADD – RIGHT-HAND BAT, OFF-BREAK BOWLER

Born: Whitestone, Hereford, 27 October 1933

*Portrait of John Chadd.*

First-class matches for Worcestershire: 2
- versus Scotland, Hamilton Crescent, Glasgow, 21, 23, 24 May 1955
- versus Oxford University, New Road, Worcester, 30 June 2, 3 July 1956

Innings: 1; Not out: 0; Runs: 4; Highest score: 4; Caught: 1; Wickets: 2; Best bowling: 2-84

*Against Scotland, Worcestershire won by 197 runs. Declaring on 382-4, there were centuries for George Dews (105) and Bob*

*Broadbent (106), with Scotland being dismissed for 256, with James Aitchison scoring 81 and Jack Mendl 59. Martin Horton took 5-52 for the visitors.*

*Declaring on 174-3 (Don Kenyon 94 and Laddie Outschoorn 56), Worcestershire set Scotland 301 to win but they fell short being bowled out for 103 with Reg Perks claiming 7-32. Chadd did not bat in either innings and bowled a total of just six overs in the game.*

*Against Oxford University, Worcestershire won by 131 runs. Worcestershire were dismissed for 294 with half-centuries for captain Peter Richardson (58) and George Dews (94). In the only innings of his first-class career, Chadd was run out for 4.*

*Oxford declared on 252-9 thanks to 71 from Peter Delisle and 64 not out from Michael Eagar with Chadd claiming the wickets of Aubrey Walshe and Victor Clube, the noted astrophysicist who has an asteroid named after him. In their second innings Worcestershire declared on 184-5 with a second half-century for Dews (62), setting the students 227 to win. In an innings lasting 38.1 overs, Oxford were bowled out for just 95 thanks to Len Coldwell (3-33) and Martin Horton (4-19).*

*Brian Hall was also making his debut for Worcestershire in this game and features elsewhere in this publication.*

After leaving Hereford Cathedral School in 1951, Chadd was called up for national service in February the following year. He spent most of his time in Egypt which he enjoyed as it allowed him the opportunity to play cricket out there. When he came out of the RAF he went into the family business, Chadds of Hereford Ltd, a drapery store business in Commercial Street started by his father, William Chadd, in 1929.

*Chadds of Hereford.*

At weekends, Chadd played his cricket for Hereford City and has maintained his connections with Herefordshire and Worcestershire cricket to this day. He also represented the Gentlemen of Herefordshire, pictured here in a game at New Road, Worcester. Chadd is standing (second from the right) behind Guy Thornycroft and the captain is H.T.H. Foley, both of whom appear elsewhere in this publication.

*Gentlemen of Herefordshire in the game played at New Road, Worcester.*

After two successful seasons Chadd was invited to play in a trial game at New Road in August 1954. He recalls: '*Major Maurice Jewell, who was Worcestershire president at that time came out to umpire. When I started to bowl, luckily I managed to turn a few off breaks with the result that I was offered a contract for the following season.*'

Representing the second XI in 1955, Chadd showed promise with figures of 4-59 against Gloucestershire and 6-56 against

Glamorgan. A first-team debut was made in the game against Scotland with Chadd recalling one vivid memory of the great Worcestershire character of the time, Roly Jenkins.

*'Against Scotland Roly had a long bowl against their star batsman, the Rev Jimmy Aitchison. The reverend gentleman infuriated Roly by frequently sweeping him, often top edging him just out of the reach of the fielders. When Aitchison was finally dismissed for 81, Roly said to him in a loud voice: 'Vicar, with your bloody luck you should have been the Archbishop of Canterbury by now.'*

Chadd continued to play second XI games in 1956 plus matches against The RAF and for Worcestershire's Club and Ground team against Surrey Optimists. His second – and what proved to be final first-class appearance – came in the game against Oxford University. Once more, Roly Jenkins looms large when Chadd talks about this game.

*'I was batting with Roly when the new ball was taken. While the umpire was handing the new ball to the bowler, Roly came down the wicket to me and said that he was going to hit the first ball for six. Sure enough he struck it into the pavilion seats, but the next ball he hit it straight to cover, called me for a run and I was run out by yards!'*

When Chadd left the staff at the end of the 1956 season he went back into the family business and played for Hereford at the weekend whom he captained for 20 seasons from 1960 to 1980. During that period they won the Three Counties League eight times, and in 1965, along with Brian Smith and Keith Edwards, Chadd took 100 wickets in the season.

Their great rivals were Worcester City who had a similar record. They were captained by Chadd 's great friend and Worcestershire stalwart John Elliott, who would greet Chadd with the same remark before every match they played: *'Hi Chaddy, no talking until after the game!'* Both sides had players with first-class experience and Worcester notably had Doug Slade who was probably both the best batsman and bowler in the League.

Chadd is pictured as captain of Hereford City Sports Club in 1977 when they were Three Counties League Challenge Winners. Steve Watkins is on the back row, second from the left. He also appears elsewhere in this publication.

*Captain of Hereford Sports Club in 1977.*

Chadd made three more appearances for Worcestershire second XI and has one final recollection of his time: *'I remember playing against Northants at Redditch. Whenever we played Northants the rumour was that Frank Tyson was playing and this time he was. He bowled very quickly as he had to in order to prove his fitness. He did, though, keep the ball well up to the relief of all our team with the exception of the super-confident Dick Richardson who asked him none too politely: "Is that the fastest you can bowl?" He went on to score a quick half-century against him and finished up with 109.'*

Chadd's involvement in cricket continued throughout this time; he served on the committee at Worcestershire CCC from 1988 until 2004 when the Club was re-constituted. He states that the most rewarding time was as chairman of cricket from 1995 to 1998. *'I had the pleasure of working with two fine cricketers and fine men, coach David Houghton and captain Tom Moody.'*

The contribution which Chadd has made to Herefordshire and Worcestershire cricket cannot be underestimated. He served as president of Herefordshire CCC from 1995 until 2004 and also president of the Midland Cricket Club Conference between 1988 and 1999.

In addition, Chadd was made a vice-president of Worcestershire CCC in 2000 and for the start of the 2003 season the players could be seen wearing the new striped Sunday blazers ... courtesy of Chadds of Hereford.

*Worcestershire CCC squad from 2003.*

The following year Chadd retired as managing director of Chadds after 50 years of working for the store. He enjoyed holidays in Barbados and watching cricket at New Road, and held the prestigious post of club president in 2006 and 2007.

The cricketing family traditions continue. As well as following the fortunes of Worcestershire and Herefordshire, Chadd visits Burghill and Tillington Cricket Club, where two of his grandchildren play and where his son-in-law is the coach. His daughter, Kirsty Sockett, is the finance and administration officer for Herefordshire Cricket.

# CHATHAM

## CHARLES HENRY CHATHAM – RIGHT-HAND BAT, RIGHT-ARM MEDIUM PACE

Born: Tewkesbury, Gloucestershire, 18 June 1910
Died: Cheltenham, Gloucestershire, 24 February 1994

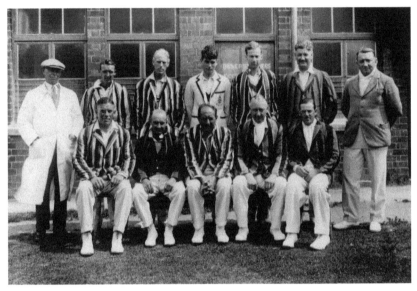

*Gentlemen of Worcestershire – Charles Chatham is standing, second from the left.*

First-class matches for Worcestershire: 1 versus Oxford University, The Parks, Oxford, 5, 7, 8 May 1934

Innings: 2; Not out: 0; Runs: 12; Highest score: 8; Caught: 0; Wickets: 1; Best bowling: 1-49

*Match drawn. Batting first, Worcestershire were bowled out for 299 with former Oxford student, the elegant Nawab of Pataudi, holding the innings together with 126. Oxford replied with 377 thanks to 118 from David Walker and half-centuries from 'Mandy'*

*Mitchell-Innes (69) and Edward Moss (50). Tragically both Walker and Moss – who was awarded the DFC in 1944 – were to lose their lives in World War Two. Moss was Charles Chatham's sole first-class wicket when he was caught behind by Edward Baker.*

*Worcestershire declared their second innings on 246-8 with half-centuries from 'Doc' Gibbons (93) and Pataudi (56). Requiring 169 to win, the students closed on 94-2.*

Charles Chatham's father, Charles Edwin Chatham, was a local Gloucestershire butcher and farmed the land at Grange Farm, Bredon. It was he who instilled a love of country pursuits and cricket in his son.

*Charles (on the left) with his father,*
*on White Hall I and White Hall II at Grange Farm.*

During his education at Wycliffe College in Gloucestershire, Chatham became lifelong friends with classmate Charlie Barnett, the great Gloucestershire opening bat. Barnett used Gunn and Moore bats and when he had no further use for them, would send them back to the manufacturer to have them re-bladed. They would then find their way to Charles for him to use.

Chatham always attended the old boys annual cricket match at Wycliffe and would help the young cricketers there with net practice and coaching, passing on his cricketing wisdom, a gesture which was always appreciated.

*A young Chatham from his school days –*
*back row, extreme right.*

Chatham played for Gloucester Gypsies – one of the first 'wandering sides' – the Gentlemen of Herefordshire, the Gentlemen of Worcestershire and the Cotswold Hunt XI. In spite of representing a range of teams he would still find time to play for his local club sides Tewkesbury and Cheltenham. They would play against opposition such as Warwickshire Imps and local rivals Evesham.

*Truman Howell*

**THE GENTLEMEN OF HEREFORDSHIRE**

(Seated) Captain R. Wood Power, Mr. Foley, Colonel M. Thorneycroft, Mr. R. F. Abbott and Mr. S. T. Freeman. (Standing) Umpire, Messrs. J. Goodwin, S. Morris, C. H. Chatham, C. F. Cox, D. A. Cocks, H. A. Picton and E. E. Morris

*Chatham, back row in the striped blazer. On the front row, second from the left, is H.T.H. Foley who appears elsewhere in this publication.*

*Dennis Moss*

**THE COTSWOLD HUNT CRICKET XI.**

The side which beat the Beaufort Hunt in the recent match played in Stowell Park, Cheltenham, by 77 runs in the kind of cricket that is far more restful than the Test sort The names are: (l. to r., standing) J. Leech, F. Lewis, J. S. Wood, C. Chatham, J. Talbot, T. Serman, N. Haywood, and C. Haywood; (sitting) T. D. Hood, B. Margrett, C. R. Heber-Percy, M.F.H. (Cotswold), and J. Hitch

*Chatham standing in the middle at the back in his customary striped blazer.*

In 1930 Chatham had county trials and played for Gloucestershire seconds. The County wanted him to play more regularly but he could not afford to give up farming. He was presented with the 'cricket or farming' option as a career, and continued with his farming.

On 19 July 1934 Charles Chatham played in a Walter Hammond benefit game for Ullenwood and Witcombe against Mr A.T. Voyce's XI – a side which included Hammond, Tom Goddard, Reg Sinfield, Billy Neale and Charlie Parker, a man who took 3,278 first-class wickets! They declared on 130-6, although Ullenwood and Witcombe were dismissed for just 20. During the game Chatham was called on to bowl to Hammond, whom he dismissed with his underarm lobs but not before Hammond had struck 46 including five sixes and two fours.

A keen horseman and breeder, Chatham raced at point-to-point meetings and rode with the Croome Estate and North Cotswold Hunts to 'show' those that had been bred. His expertise was further in evidence when, on occasion, he would 'ride out' with the great national hunt trainers, Fred and Mercy Rimell, and 'Frenchie' Nicholson, father of the great trainer David 'The Duke' Nicholson. He once 'rode under rules' wearing his colours of pink with silver stars; in those days the jockey would own the colours.

Speaking to Charles's son, Richard, he told me that: *'In 1936 Dad took over the 100-acre Manor Farm in Tredington near Tewkesbury. Having previously lived in Bredon, Worcestershire, this residential qualification had allowed him to play for the County in 1934. He started the Tredington herd of British Friesians, a home grown and carefully bred pedigree, award-winning herd. As a family we took the herd on to great heights until the EU membership destroyed the milk industry. We then redeveloped the farm into the award-winning Sherdons Golf Centre.'*

He was equally keen on his amateur dramatics with Bredon Players and it was during a production at Watson Hall in

Tewkesbury that he met his wife Marjorie, who was visiting a friend at the time.

A senior Air Raid Precautions warden during the War, Chatham continued to serve the County. He became a JP – the youngest in the country at the time – chairman of the juvenile bench in Tewkesbury and then chairman of the licensing bench.

His community work was recognised in July 1963 when the *Gloucestershire Echo* printed a picture of him receiving a long-service medal from Cheltenham Rural District Civil Defence. His work continued as a county councillor and chairman of the Tewkesbury National Farmers Union and Young Farmers. In addition, he was a church warden, chairman of the parish council and a county councillor.

As a youngster, Charles had developed an interest in flying, having witnessed as a very small boy the exploits of Colonel Samuel Cody and his flying circus. In 1929 he attended the Schneider Trophy contest while visiting relatives in Southampton.

*Programme from the Schneider Trophy contest in 1929.*

This passion for flying was never more evident than in 1981 when he wanted to go to Canada to visit family but was unwell. He struggled with osteoarthritis in later life which was brought on by a fall from a horse who hesitated at a fence and, as his son Richard says, *'he exited by the front door'*.

As an alternative, a trip on Concorde was arranged with a flight over The Bay of Biscay. Charles is seen here about to board the plane, proudly wearing his Gloucester Gypsies tie.

*Charles Chatham about to board Concorde.*

His passion for flying was handed down to his son Richard, an authority and lecturer nationwide on Concorde.

# COLLINSON

## JOHN COLLINSON – RIGHT-HAND BAT, OFF-BREAK BOWLER

Born: Sotterley, Suffolk, 2 October 1911
Died: Hove, Sussex, 29 August 1979

*John Collinson (right) with Worcestershire players Alan Duff (left) and George Chesterton (centre), taken at Lancing College, West Sussex.*

First-class matches for Worcestershire: 1 versus Combined Services, New Road, Worcester, 31 July, 1, 2 August 1946

Innings: 2; Not out: 0; Runs: 24; Highest score: 23; Caught: 0; Did not bowl

*Combined Services won by five wickets thanks to 107 by Don Kenyon and half-centuries from Mike Ainsworth (50 not out) and Reg Perks (51) all of whom ironically played for Worcestershire. Collinson scored 23 in Worcestershire's first innings before he became one of Dick Pollard's four victims. Norman Bennett and Dennis Good were also making their debuts for Worcestershire in this game and feature elsewhere in this publication.*

52

John Collinson began playing cricket while at St John's School, Leatherhead. By 1939 he was making appearances for Middlesex second XI and on 14 August scored 62 and 36 not out against Surrey at Ealing. This earned him his first-class debut the following week versus Gloucestershire at Cheltenham, where he scored 34 and 13 in a heavy, 186-run defeat.

He retained his place for the following game against Somerset at Lord's, where he scored 19 in each innings as Middlesex won by 225 runs. Collinson opened with Jack Robertson, and the top six, apart from Collinson, comprised England Test batsmen – Jack Robertson, Bill Edrich, Denis Compton, George Mann and Walter Robins.

Between 1941 and 1945, Collinson made 23 appearances for the British Empire XI, a team set up to raise funds for the Red Cross in a series of charity matches; 243 games were played in total. Collinson played alongside big names such as Keith Miller, Trevor Bailey, Ken Cranston and the Bedser twins, and had a top score of 52 against the Metropolitan Police at Imber Court in 1942.

In 1943 he appeared twice for Sussex in one-day games against the RAF and United Services plus two appearances for the Lord's XI against Surrey Colts in 1943 and 1944.

*John Collinson batting.*

In 1944–45 he played five times for the Birmingham Festival XI in fundraising games at Edgbaston against Sussex, Northants and three games against the RAF. He played alongside Learie Constantine, Walter Hammond, Bob Wyatt, Reg Simpson and Eric Hollies, and made a top score of 24 not out against Northants.

It was at this time that Collinson wrote a regular feature titled 'To help you think', for *The Cricketer* magazine, for which he would write at length about the technical aspects of the game.

During the War, Collinson was a maths teacher and cricket coach at Cranleigh School. In a history of the school during the War years he was described as *'surely the best player we have ever had here. Mr. Collinson, by his single-minded enthusiasm for the game and his painstaking coaching – together with a number of promising cricketers – raised the standard of cricket at Cranleigh to a higher level than for many years past.'*

An appointment followed at Malvern College which encompassed the role of master in charge of cricket. By 1949, however, there were murmurings from some of the influential 'Old Malvernians' that, aligned to some poor performances, the traditional Malvern standard of attacking cricket had subsided into the doldrums. Their spokesman was the highly respected former England batsman and captain of Surrey, Errol Holmes.

In his book *A Remarkable Man – The Story of George Chesterton*, former Hampshire all-rounder Andy Murtagh quotes from the letter which Holmes submitted to headmaster Tom Gaunt: '*We always believed that Collinson is not the right man to hold the position of cricket master. The tradition at Malvern has always been to attack, because that is the best method of defence. Whoever takes on the role must believe wholeheartedly in this theory and is someone who will instil in the boys the fact that the bat is provided for the purpose of hitting the ball, not as a weapon of defence.*' His closing comments were that these principles were foreign to Collinson.

To his credit, Collinson had outlined as early as the summer of 1946 that: '*It will probably be as much as three years before we can be confident of producing good players and good teams comparable to pre-War standards. There had been no first-class cricket so boys had had no opportunity to watch and copy their heroes.*' He continued: '*They had to travel far and wide for nets and practice games, and when they were there, few able and willing masters were on hand to help and to coach. Add all that to the absence of a normal number of 16- and 17-year-olds.*'

While Collinson defended himself, he was relieved of his duties as cricket master by George Chesterton. In a letter from the headmaster to Errol Holmes he sensitively addressed how he solved the problem, allowing Collinson to 'save face': '*My dear Holmes, I am writing to you to tell you that Collinson has today asked me, in view of his considerable duties as a housemaster, to relieve him of his commitments as master in charge of cricket at Malvern. I have agreed to this and asked G.H. Chesterton to take his place.*' Collinson continued with his teaching and housemaster duties and spent much of his spare time on the golf course.

Although Collinson had had his detractors at Malvern, many believed that he was not a bad man and was far from being an inefficient, third-rate schoolmaster. These people also believed that he had fine qualities as a teacher, not least an overwhelming concern for his pupils.

Regarded as being too intense, Collinson desperately wanted his boys to do well but was unable to prevent himself from communicating this anxiety and tension to those in charge. The boys would sense this and, in their eagerness not to let him down, would get anxious and fail to do themselves justice.

It was known that he had financial problems and as a mathematician believed he could play the stock market. In the end the pressure got too much and he cracked. He became a sad figure and dropped out of sight when he left Malvern; thereafter, he led a solitary life.

# DAVIDGE

## GUY MORTIMER COLERIDGE DAVIDGE – RIGHT-HAND BATSMAN

Born: Woolwich, Kent, 2 March 1878
Died: Hove, Sussex, 17 February 1956

*Portrait of Guy Davidge.*

First-class matches for Worcestershire: 1 versus Oxford University, The Parks, Oxford, 25, 26, 27 May 1911

Innings: 1; Not out: 0; Runs: 0; Highest score: 0; Caught: 1; Did not bowl

*Worcestershire won by six wickets. Oxford were dismissed for 313 (Freddie Knott 66 not out and Richard Twining 57) with Worcestershire replying with 359. Davidge was one of Claude Burton's four wickets who had him bowled without score in what was his only first-class innings. The visitors were indebted to George Simpson-Hayward for his 130, scored in precisely two hours, an innings which contained 17 fours and two sixes.*

*Thanks to a second four-wicket haul from Bill Taylor (4-88 and 4-40) plus Ted Arnold with 3-29, the students were dismissed for just 140. Davidge's contribution was a catch to dismiss Robert Braddell for 10. Finishing on 95-4 with Arnold 63 not out, Worcestershire got home comfortably.*

*Major Davis and Frederick Burr were also making their debuts for Worcestershire in this game and feature elsewhere in this publication.*

Guy Davidge's father, deputy surgeon-general John Davidge, had an outstanding military career of nearly 60 years. Such was his influence that his son was to follow in his footsteps, also pursuing a lifelong military career.

Davidge spent the first two years of his life living in Woolwich and then lived in Malta where his father was serving as a Brigade Surgeon with the Malta Garrison. They returned to Portsmouth in October 1885 for Davidge to begin his education, firstly at Newton College, Newton Abbot and then Malvern College. There he enjoyed his sport, especially athletics and tennis, of which he was regarded as a first-class player.

Having undertaken his cadetship at the Royal Military Academy, Sandhurst, Davidge was commissioned as second lieutenant in the Worcestershire Regiment on 16 February 1898 and promoted to lieutenant on 10 January 1900.

At Edgbaston in May 1910 Davidge represented Worcestershire second XI in a two-day match against Warwickshire seconds. Scores of 24 not out and 10 were not enough to save the visitors from an innings and 60-run defeat. In June 1911 a repeat of the fixture yielded a similar result, a 252-run defeat. Davidge fared better with the bat, scoring 31 and 42 before being dismissed in each innings by Frederick Clark.

In Warwickshire's second innings of 215-2 declared, Davidge claimed his only wicket for Worcestershire, dismissing Stanley Richardson for 12. Later in the season, playing for the Gentlemen of Worcestershire, he demonstrated his batting prowess, scoring 108 against Bromsgrove School and 174 against the Warwickshire Gentlemen. He also made appearances for his local side, St John's, in Worcester.

Davidge continued to serve as a subaltern in the Mounted Infantry of the 2nd Battalion in the South African Boer War, taking part in the fighting at Slingersfontein. Between 1911 and 1912 he served with the 1st Battalion on the Isle of Wight and was appointed adjutant of the 7th Battalion at Kidderminster, where he was stationed when War broke out in 1914.

Having headed to France in April 1915 with the 7th Battalion, Davidge took command of the 3rd Battalion later in the year. The first big engagement came in the spring of 1916 at Vimy Ridge. Reports state that: *'Throughout this fighting Colonel Davidge proved on many occasions his moral courage, no less than his physical bravery and determination and despite more than 300 casualties, the confidence of the men in their leader was never shaken.'*

At Ovillers the good leadership of Colonel Davidge had decisive results with the 3rd Battalion seizing and holding a trench junction near Pozieres. On July 13, however, before the village actually surrendered, Colonel Davidge himself was hit and badly wounded.

In March 1917 he returned to France, this time to the 1st Battalion, and taking over command he was sent north to Passchendaele. Following the fierce fighting on the first day, he was awarded the Distinguished Service Order (DSO) on 9 January, the citation in *The London Gazette* reading: *(Acting lieutenant-Colonel) Guy Mortimer Coleridge Davidge, Worcester*

*Regiment – For conspicuous gallantry and devotion to duty. When the right flank of his brigade had become exposed, he was ordered to form a defensive flank with his battalion. This he did with the utmost skill and success, thereby enabling the troops on his left to maintain the ground they had gained. He visited the position taken by the battalion under very heavy machine gun and shell fire, displaying splendid coolness and disregard of personal safety.'*

In the winter, Davidge's health broke down and he was invalided home where he commanded a young soldiers' battalion of the King's Own Yorkshire Light Infantry.

By March 1918 he was back in the thick of the action, this time in the face of ferocious fighting in and around the Aisne in Northern France. Fighting a continuous series of rearguard actions, the remnants of three British divisions were driven back. The fighting continued for three days and nights, during which time Colonel Davidge miraculously escaped death or capture. For his action he received a bar to his DSO and was mentioned in despatches on three occasions.

The citation for his bar read: *'For conspicuous gallantry and devotion to duty in action. He handled his battalion in a remarkably cool and resourceful way, and frequently anticipated orders according to the exigencies of the situation in difficult conditions. Again, later, he did particularly gallant and soldierly work, freely exposing himself to heavy fire and maintaining a close grip of the situation. It was due to his fine behaviour that his part of the line remained intact.'*

It proved to be Davidge's last action because on 30 May he was badly wounded once more, this time by a shell. He was invalided home until after the War and once he had recovered re-joined the 3rd Battalion as second in command until November 1921, when he took over command of the 2nd Battalion in Dublin.

*2nd Battalion cricket team from the mid-1920s.*

Colonel Davidge commanded the 2nd Battalion from 1921 to 1925, when he retired. During this spell he found time to represent the 2nd Battalion first XI cricket team, pictured here. He is seated third from the left. The picture includes Worcestershire players Lieutenant 'Bobbie' Burlton (seated second from the left) and Captain Geoffrey Sheppard (seated second from the right). Sheppard appears elsewhere in this publication.

# DAVIS

## MAJOR DAVIS – RIGHT-HAND BAT, WICKET-KEEPER

Born: Lye, Stourbridge, Worcestershire, 27 March 1882
Died: Blakebrook, Kidderminster, Worcestershire, 27 April 1959

*Major Davis in the mid-1940s.*

First-class matches for Worcestershire: 1 versus Oxford University, The Parks, Oxford, 25, 26, 27 May 1911

Innings: 2; Not out: 0; Runs: 35; Highest score: 29; Caught: 1; Did not bowl

*Worcestershire won by six wickets. Oxford were dismissed for 313 with Worcestershire replying with 359. Davis was one of Claude Burton's four wickets and had him caught for 29. The visitors were indebted to George Simpson-Hayward for his 130, scored in precisely two hours, an innings which contained 17 fours and two sixes.*

*Thanks to a second four-wicket haul from Bill Taylor (4-88 and 4-40) plus Ted Arnold with 3-29, the students were dismissed for just 140. Davis's contribution was a catch to dismiss Oxford's captain, John Evans (whose brother, W.H.B. Evans played for Worcestershire in 1901) off the bowling of Arthur Conway for 37. Finishing on 95-4 with Arnold 63 not out, Worcestershire got home comfortably.*

*Guy Davidge and Frederick Burr were also making their debuts for Worcestershire in this game and feature elsewhere in this publication.*

Major Davis's father, John, was the foreman at a firm of chain makers from the Black Country and lived on High Street in Lye with his four sons and two daughters. Major Davis's brother, John Percy Davis, a keen cricketer, played for Stourbridge in the Birmingham League and made four first-class appearances for Worcestershire in 1922.

*Stourbridge CC in 1942. John Davis is seated on the extreme right, still playing in his late-50s.*

Major Davis and three of his brothers – John A. Davis, John P. Davis and Edgar Davis – worked for the railways and in Major Davis's case, spent his entire working life in that profession. The register of clerks shows that he joined the Great Western Railway on 1 October 1896 in the goods department at Stourbridge Station. Andrew Jones, a Great Western Railway historian told me:

*'Gaining a situation as a junior clerk was dependent on a number of factors. Firstly, before setting foot in a railway office, prospective clerks would have been required to provide security and present testimonials written by respectable individuals who could attest to their good character.*

*'Secondly, the majority of railways expected these individuals to pass exams. Therefore, because of the necessary conditions – money and education – in order to become a junior clerk, the majority would have had middle-class backgrounds.'*

Once Davis had passed the rigorous entrance procedures he immediately received benefits, starting on a higher salary than other railway employees.

By March 1906 his career was progressing. Rather than having a job which entailed general duties, he became a goods clerk in the District Goods Manager's Office. Information from the Great Western Railway indicates that he was making his way up the pay scale and was given more day-to-day responsibilities.

A keen sportsman, Davis's skill as a wicket-keeper-batsman was shining through, his cricketing exploits being reported in the local press. In May 1907, playing for Stourbridge against Walsall, the *County Advertiser and Herald for Staffordshire* and *Worcester* stated: *'Special mention should be made of Major Davis behind the wickets. He was smart in taking the ball and did a fine piece of work in stumping Hurst.'*

He continued to progress and in May 1909 made his debut for Worcestershire second XI against Warwickshire second XI in a two-day game at Edgbaston, which resulted in a seven-wicket defeat for Worcestershire. While scoring only eight and nought he did take two catches, helping to dismiss Warwickshire's Russell Everitt. (Everitt also played for Worcestershire and appears elsewhere in this publication.)

In the return fixture at New Road in August, Warwickshire seconds were to win by the margin of 11 wickets in a 12-a-side game, Davis being dismissed for scores of five and 16.

By this time, Davis's career on the railways had progressed and he was working in Bilston where he was involved in the setting up of the Bilston Goods Division which was being built at the time.

His third and final outing for Worcestershire seconds was in a two-day game starting on 16 May 1910, once more against Warwickshire at Edgbaston. On this occasion the home side was victorious by an innings and 60 runs. In Worcestershire's first innings of 150, Davis acquitted himself well, his 25 being second-top score in the innings; however, the visitors were dismissed for just 83 in their second innings, resulting in a heavy defeat.

Despite the lack of success with Worcestershire, Davis continued to excel for Stourbridge. *The Dudley Chronicle* of 4 June 1910 reported his score of 82 for Stourbridge versus Kidderminster in the Birmingham League game at Kidderminster. The report read: *'He added 80 with his brother but Major played by far his best innings. He helped himself to 18 off one over from H. Tomkinson including a lovely straight drive out of the ground for 6.'*

A fortnight later, better was to follow in the game against Mitchells and Butlers at Cape Hill, a score of 58. Thomas Clare, who played two matches for Worcestershire in the 1920s, wrote for the *Dudley Chronicle*: *'The feature of the afternoon's cricket was a splendid first-wicket stand for Stourbridge where Major Davis completed another brilliant half-century. With three successive half-centuries, we shall have to call Major the Stourbridge wonder. He is certainly batting at the top of his form and is worthy of trial in the County eleven.'*

On 30 July Davis carried his bat for 46 not out as Stourbridge were bowled out for 119 in response to Dudley's 227-2 declared.

Davis also played hockey, in the League for Dudley and for Worcestershire against Staffordshire in early November in Wolverhampton. His agility as a wicket-keeper was in play but on this occasion he was in goal. On 26 November the *County Express* reported that: *'Major Davis, the Worcestershire hockey goalkeeper, did splendid work for his county against Staffordshire.'*

In February 1911 Davis kept goal for the Midlands against the South in the international trial hockey match at Bournville. The report in the *County Express* stated: *'Keeping goal for Midlands is Major Davis, who if they win the game will be international trial champions for the first time. After the game the England team will be selected. It is hoped Major Davis will catch the eye of the selectors.'* Sadly, the international call-up did not materialise.

Davis made a fine start to the 1911 cricket season, with the *Dudley Chronicle* reporting on Stourbridge's home game against Handsworth Wood on 27 May. *'Opening with Thomas Clare two records for league cricket on the ground were broken. Firstly, Clare scored 105 in an hour,'* an innings akin to one played by Gilbert Jessop, *'and secondly, with Major Davis (46), they put on 150 for the first wicket in under an hour as they chased down 201 to win for the loss of just two wickets.'*

In August Davis scored a well-crafted 62 in the defeat against Kidderminster, the match summary stating: *'Two lovely leg-side strokes off Alec Skelding both produced boundaries and drew loud cheers from a fair company of spectators.'* He was, however, later given out for obstructing the field.

Davis was appointed Club captain for 1913 which was reported in the *Dudley Chronicle's* pre-season write-up headed 'Major the new skip': '*A wonderful hockey player in his day but an even better cricketer. "Keeps sticks" in county style and "bags 'em neatly" on both sides and whips off the bails in a twinkling. A thoroughly reliable bat with a pose which beggars description. It isn't the pose that gets runs, it's Major's masterly manipulation of the willow.'* Outgoing captain Jack Hingley summed up the appointment by stating that '*No better choice could have been made. He knows the game from A-Z.'*

*At the seaside with his family. Major Davis is on the left.*

Having married Hilda Humphries in April 1912 (she was to die in 1945; he subsequently married Phyllis Bridges in 1947), Davis continued to work on the railways, living in Birmingham and working as a railway manager representative. He continued to play cricket, moving to Old Hill where he played in the second team well into his 40s.

Into his early 50s and still playing the occasional game of cricket, in August 1932 Davis represented the Gentlemen of Worcestershire in a two-day game at New Road, Worcester, versus The Queries, a holiday touring side. While the *Birmingham Mail* reported a quiet game for Davis, the headline next to it, covering the Worcestershire versus Nottinghamshire fixture, made for more interesting reading: 'Collapse against Larwood' as he ran through the Worcestershire batting claiming nine wickets!

*Major Davis with his wife Phyllis.*

In his retirement, Davis would visit New Road to watch the first team play. Sitting at the Diglis End of the ground he proved a popular figure; with rationing still in force he would bring plums from his garden to share with other spectators.

# EVERITT

## RUSSELL STANLEY EVERITT – RIGHT-HAND BAT, RIGHT-ARM MEDIUM, OCCASIONAL WICKET-KEEPER

Born: King's Heath, Birmingham, Warwickshire, 8 September 1881
Died: Kew Gardens, Surrey, 11 May 1973

*Portrait of Russell Everitt.*

First-class matches for Worcestershire: 1 versus Cambridge University, Fenner's, Cambridge, 30, 31 May, 1 June 1901

Innings: 2; Not out: 1; Runs: 6; Highest score: 6 not out; Caught: 0; Did not bowl

*Cambridge University won by seven wickets. Having won the toss and elected to bat, Worcestershire were bowled out for 167 and were spared embarrassment thanks to half-centuries from 'Dick' Pearson (60) and Charles Corden (51 not out). Batting at number seven, Everitt was dismissed for a duck, one of seven wickets for Rockley Wilson.*

*Dismissing the students for 271 (Sammy Day 76 and Edward Dowson 97), George Wilson claimed four wickets and there were three apiece for Pearson and Albert Bird. In their second innings, Worcestershire were bowled out for 203 with only Percy Francis (66) showing much resistance. Once again, Wilson was the pick of the bowlers, returning figures of 7-38. The students reached their target of 100 for the loss of just three wickets.*

Russell Everitt was the youngest of six children. His father, Frederick, a JP, owned the brewery F. Everitt and Company – Maltsters of King's Heath in Birmingham. In 1888 he took over Isaac Bates's Brewery in High Street, King's Heath, renaming it the King's Heath Brewery. It was sold by Everitt in 1896 when it was acquired by Birmingham Breweries Ltd.

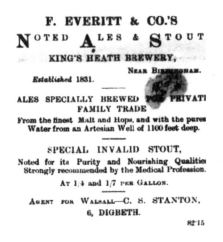

*Brewery advertisement for F. Everitt and Company.*

*The King's Heath Brewery.*

Aged 12, Russell Everitt's cricketing prowess was evident when he took eight wickets for his prep school, The Uplands, as the opposition, Arden House, were bowled out for 21. Later, Everitt attended Malvern College from 1895 until 1900, but did not make the cricket XI.

By the turn of the century the family was living in the Worcestershire village of Barnt Green for whom Everitt played between 1898 and 1901. He also represented other Midlands sides, such as Stratford-upon-Avon, Olton and King's Heath. His best performance for Barnt Green was in the match against Selly Oak in July 1900 when he took six wickets as the home side were dismissed for just 45 runs.

A keen sportsman, Everitt represented Worcestershire at hockey in 1901 and played billiards for Birmingham the following year.

After initial employment on leaving school in the family brewing business, in 1902 he went to gain further experience of the industry by working in the accounts department of Mitchells and Butlers, the well-known Midlands brewing company.

Following his first-class debut for Worcestershire in 1901, Everitt played occasional games for Warwickshire second XI and Club and Ground teams from 1902 onwards. In 1908, playing for Moseley in the Birmingham and District League, he headed the averages with 710 runs at 54.62.

He made his County Championship debut for Warwickshire against Surrey at The Oval in 1909. Everitt was surprisingly made captain when the regular skipper, Alf Glover, was taken ill. The *Birmingham Mail* regarded it as a '*strange decision*' especially as the experienced Test wicket-keeper, 'Dick' Lilley, was in the team. Surrey won by 171 runs.

The *Birmingham Daily Post* described the action stating that: '*The Warwickshire batting was extremely disappointing. With 33 runs still needed to avoid the follow on – and only three wickets in hand – Messrs Everitt and Foster came together and by an unexpected exhibition of pluck and resolution saved the situation. They stayed together for an hour and not only averted the indignity of a follow on but added 60 runs for the eighth wicket.'*

Everitt played in the next two games, firstly against Derbyshire and then the return fixture with Surrey at Edgbaston. Despite catching Jack Hobbs in the second innings, he witnessed 'The Master's' four innings of: 41, 159, 160 and 100 at close quarters.

By 1910 Everitt had moved to London and was living in Hampstead and working as an accountant for the Courage Brewery. He then changed roles to become a wine merchant and manager, looking after tenanted pubs. At Lord's, in the August of 1910, he played for Hampstead against MCC. In an innings and 31-run defeat, he had the satisfaction of bowling the highly influential figure of Lord Hawke for 22.

Following the outbreak of War, in April 1915 Everitt paid to join the Honorary Artillery Corps and was a member of the 2nd Battalion, quickly rising to the rank of sergeant. He was then fast tracked to a commission and in October 1916 took the post of second lieutenant of the 102nd Machine Gun Corps with this unit in France. He then joined the 5th Royal North Lancashire Regiment in August 1917 as a second lieutenant, serving overseas until May 1919.

On 11 June he appeared once more at Lord's, opening the batting for the Honourable Artillery Company against the Household Brigade who won by 109 runs. Opening the batting for the Household Brigade was Old Malvernian Herbert Gordon, who would play for Worcestershire in 1923.

Everitt married Madeline Gertrude Warner on 4 June 1921 and was living in Stevens Lane, Thames Ditton, Kew at the time;

the marriage certificate described his job as 'outside manager for a brewery'. He continued to play cricket for Richmond into the mid-1920s including a game against The Bank of England in June 1923. The 1939 census shows that he was living in Claygate, Esher. His occupation is quoted as brewery manager.

# FAWCUS

## CHARLES LESLIE DINSDALE FAWCUS – LEFT-HAND BAT, LEFT-ARM MEDIUM

Born: Bromley, Kent, 8 December 1898
Died: Worthing, Sussex, 8 December 1967

*Leslie Fawcus in cricket whites.*

First-class matches for Worcestershire: 1 versus Oxford University, The Parks, Oxford, 20, 21, 22 May 1925

Innings: 2; Not out: 0; Runs: 47; Highest score: 43; Caught: 0; Wickets: 0; Best bowling: 0-6

*Match drawn. Winning the toss and electing to bat, the students scored 364 all out thanks to Geoffrey Legge (120), John Stephenson (66) and Louis Serrurier (64 not out). Serrurier was to play for Worcestershire in 1927. Fred Root (5-120) was the pick of the Worcestershire bowlers. Worcestershire replied with 379 (Maurice Foster 68 and Herbert Hopkins 122) including 43 from Fawcus before he was run out.*

*Oxford's second innings was held together by Claude Taylor who carried his bat for 105 not out as they were dismissed for 272 with Root taking 6-83. Fawcus bowled three overs for six runs. Requiring 258 to win, Worcestershire held on for the draw, closing on 194-9, Fawcus's contribution being four before being bowled by John Greenstock. Greenstock had made his first-class debut for Worcestershire in 1924.*

*Henry Foley was also making his debut for Worcestershire in this game and features elsewhere in this publication.*

The son of Charles Octavius Fawcus, a coal merchant and shipbroker, Leslie Fawcus was educated at Bradfield College from 1909 until 1917, where he captained the football team in his final year and fives side for two years. In 1914, aged just 15, he played in the school first XI, opened the batting and headed the averages for three consecutive seasons. In 1916 he averaged 125.25 with a highest score of 164 not out. A cricketer of some quality, his *Wisden* obituary in 1968 noted that: '*He was regarded as the best batsman ever to play for Bradfield.*'

On leaving school, Fawcus joined the Royal Military Academy at Woolwich, the training school for officers in the Royal Engineers. Playing for the Royal Military Academy against Dulwich College in June 1917 he cracked 153 not out in a total of 354-5 declared. For good measure he took three wickets as the Academy won by the large margin of 239 runs. He continued his run of form with 67 and 24 not out – plus five wickets in the match – against the Royal Military Academy, Sandhurst, in July.

He left the Academy without graduating in September 1918, the school register stating that he had '*dipped below standard*'. He was, however, commissioned as a second lieutenant in the Royal Garrison Artillery the following day but did not see service overseas during the War.

He remained in the Royal Garrison Artillery after the War, was promoted to lieutenant in March 1920 and served in India in 1921. It was while serving in India that Fawcus married Kathleen Swann at St Andrew's, Ferozepur, before resigning his commission the following year.

Fawcus matriculated at Christ Church, Oxford, on 15 October 1924. He passed Responsions in the same year (examinations which had to be passed on or before admission) and he passed the first Public Examination in 1925. Between 1929 and 1931 he passed the remaining three papers to complete the requirements of the second Public Examination. He took a pass degree rather than honours and graduated with both a bachelor of arts and master of arts on 25 June 1931.

Unusual as it is to receive both degrees concurrently, Judith Curthoys the Christ Church University archivist confirms: '*I do not know why Leslie Fawcus received both degrees on the same day. It might be the case that because his BA graduation took longer than most (seven years) he was permitted to receive both degrees on the same day.*'

In addition to playing football, Fawcus also continued to play cricket. Between May and August 1924 he played three second XI games for Kent and in June he also made his only County Championship appearance for them in the 49-run defeat to Middlesex. May 1925 brought the unusual occurrence of playing for and against the same team in a first-class fixture. Firstly, he bagged a pair playing for Oxford against Middlesex, then made his sole appearance for Worcestershire against Oxford.

On 5 and 6 June he represented Christ Church in a home fixture against Eton Ramblers. In an innings and 116 run defeat, he made up for two low scores by claiming five Ramblers wickets. Sadly, he never gained his Blue at Oxford, narrowly missing out on one occasion due to ill health.

*Christ Church team, 1925. Fawcus is standing on the extreme right.*

Two more matches for Oxford followed in 1926, a four-wicket defeat to Essex at Chelmsford and a drawn game against Surrey at The Oval. Fawcus dropped Jack Hobbs who went on to score 261, and with Andrew Sandham (183) amassed 428 for Surrey's first wicket. The small consolation was that, in Oxford's second innings, Fawcus recorded his highest first-class score of 70 before being caught by Jack White off Douglas Jardine.

By 1933 Fawcus was playing Minor Counties cricket for Dorset while teaching at Durlston Court in Swanage. In the drawn game against Cornwall at Camborne he took career-best figures of 7-68 from 18 overs; however, Cornwall 'won' on first innings.

In 1934, Fawcus sold his stake in Durlston Court and moved to Winton Hall near Winchester where he was appointed headmaster in 1937.

His final game of Minor Counties cricket came in August 1938 against Devon, their side including Norman Humphries, who subsequently played seven matches for Worcestershire in 1946. On this occasion, however, it was Fawcus who shone, hitting 57, his highest Minor Counties score.

At the start of the War, Fawcus moved the Winton Hall pupils to Rugby where they joined Dunchurch School, which in 1940 become Dunchurch-Winton Hall. He was joint headmaster with Cyril Cook until 1958 and then sole head until he retired in 1960 when his cousin, Harold Fawcus, succeeded him.

Leslie Fawcus lived out the remaining years of his life in West Chiltington in Sussex. He died on his 69th birthday in 1967.

*View of Dunchurch Hall from the cricket field.*

# FOLEY

## HENRY THOMAS HAMILTON FOLEY – LEFT-HAND BAT, LEFT-ARM MEDIUM, OCCASIONAL WICKET-KEEPER

Born: Stoke Edith Park, Hereford, 25 April 1905
Died: Stoke Edith Park, Hereford, 13 December 1959

*Portrait of Tom Foley.*

First-class matches for Worcestershire: 1 versus Oxford University, The Parks, Oxford, 20, 21, 22 May 1925

Innings: 2; Not out: 1; Runs: 6; Highest score: 6; Caught: 0; Did not bowl

*Match drawn. Winning the toss and electing to bat, the students scored 364 all out thanks to Geoffrey Legge (120), John Stephenson (66) and Louis Serrurier (64 not out). Serrurier was to play for Worcestershire in 1927. Fred Root (5-120) was the pick of the Worcestershire bowlers. Worcestershire replied with 379 (Maurice Foster 68 and Herbert Hopkins 122.) Foley, batting at number nine, was caught by John Guise off the bowling of Warwickshire's Edward Hewetson for six.*

*Oxford's second innings was held together by Claude Taylor who carried his bat for 105 not out as they were dismissed for 272 with Root taking 6-83. Requiring 258 to win, Worcestershire held on for the draw closing on 194-9 with the last pair of Foley (0) and George Abell (41) at the crease.*

*Leslie Fawcus was also making his debut for Worcestershire in this game and features elsewhere in this publication.*

Tom Foley was the son of Paul Henry Hodgetts-Foley. Better known in cricketing circles as Paul Foley, he was a barrister and was called to the bar of the Inner Temple in 1881 and held the posts of high sheriff of Herefordshire, deputy lieutenant of Herefordshire and was a JP. The Foleys were a family of influence; an ancestor was speaker of the House of Commons at the turn of the 18th century.

It was Paul Foley who, in the late-1890s, was responsible for establishing Worcestershire County Cricket Club as a first-class county. He served as secretary and treasurer from 1890 until his retirement in 1909.

*Paul Foley in 1899.*

79

Educated at Eton, Tom Foley subsequently studied at Brasenose College, Oxford, where he gained a bachelor of arts degree on 18 February 1928.

After his debut game for Worcestershire in May 1925, Foley's next cricket was in June playing for Eton Ramblers against Christ Church, Oxford. He played 12 matches for Eton Ramblers, his last appearance being in 1939, and it was during these games that he occasionally kept wicket.

In 1927 Foley was commissioned into the Rifle Brigade Regiment and served with the 2nd Battalion in Colchester. The year after the death of his father in 1928, Tom Foley retired to look after the family estate in Herefordshire.

Having previously played for both the Green Jackets and Free Foresters, in 1932 Foley played Minor Counties cricket for Monmouthshire, making 10 appearances over the next two years. On 12 and 13 August 1932, in his debut game against Berkshire at Rodney Parade, Newport, he recorded his highest score of 83 not out in the 187-run defeat. Berkshire were indebted to H.E. 'Tom' Dollery who scored 115 and 105 not out; he went on to score over 24,000 first-class runs (including 50 centuries) in a 21-year career with Warwickshire.

On 24 June 1936, Foley married Helen Constance Margaret Pearson. In this magazine article which covered the society wedding, it's interesting to note that Foley's father-in-law was chairman of the Stock Exchange.

A year later, on 31 July 1937, an unusual story broke in the Worcestershire newspaper, *Berrow's Journal*, which ran the headline: 'Germany tour announced'. The reporter stated that: '*I understand that a team of Worcestershire gentlemen leaves shortly for Berlin for 10 days' cricket in the capital, Major M.F.S. Jewell will captain the team. Herr Hitler is reported to be very interested*

*The wedding of Tom Foley and Helen Pearson.*

*in the tour, for German cricket is still in the student stage and there is great desire to improve the standard of play.'* Foley was listed as one of the players but withdrew at short notice. The reasons for him not touring are unknown but perhaps they were due to the prevailing political climate in Germany.

In July 1939, less than two months before the outbreak of War, Foley played for Eton Ramblers in a series of three two-day tour matches in the Netherlands. Played at grounds in The Hague, Laren and Haarlem the visitors won all three.

Being a Regular Army Reserve officer, at the outbreak of War Foley re-joined. After a short period with the 2nd Motor Training Battalion at Tidworth he served on the staff of the 59th (Staffordshire) Motor Division headquarters and with the British

Expeditionary Force in France where he was evacuated from Dunkirk.

In 1940 Foley became master-at-arms to General 'Rusty' Eastwood who was commander of the 59th Staffordshire Infantry Division and remained with him while Major-General Eastwood was director general of the Home Guard (Northern Command) and subsequently governor of Gibraltar. Foley rose to the rank of captain in 1943 and was ultimately promoted to major.

*Major-General Eastwood and Captain H.T.H. Foley.*

Foley was awarded an MBE in 1944 and reverted to the Regular Army Reserve in 1946 before retiring on account of his age in 1956.

Like his father before him, Foley was a JP and became high sheriff of Herefordshire in 1947. He continued to play the occasional game of cricket and represented the Gentlemen of Herefordshire who played against his 'old' side, Eton Ramblers, in August 1959. The game, at the Racecourse Ground, Hereford, was drawn. Appearing in the Gents' side were John Chadd and Guy Thornycroft, both of whom appear elsewhere in this publication.

*Portrait of H.T.H. Foley.*

Foley's contribution to public life was further recognised when the Foley College in Stourbridge was built on land once owned by his ancestor, Thomas Foley, a great ironmaster from Stourbridge in the West Midlands. After dedicating the land for educational purposes, the newly built college was officially opened by Foley himself in September 1956. In later years it became known as The Stourbridge College of Technology and Art. Henry Foley died at the early age of 54 in December 1959.

Foley's son, Sir John Paul Foley, has continued many of the family traditions. He joined the SAS during his national service, was commissioned into the Rifle Brigade and rose to become director of the SAS in 1983. He was later director of general intelligence during the Gulf War in 1990 and became commander of British Forces in Hong Kong in 1991, before being named chief of defence intelligence in 1994. He retired from the forces in 1997.

From 2000 until 2005 he was lieutenant-governor of Guernsey, and after retiring to Herefordshire he was appointed high sheriff of Herefordshire and Worcestershire in 2006 and vice-lieutenant of Herefordshire in 2010.

# GOOD

## DENNIS CUNLIFFE GOOD – RIGHT-HAND BAT, RIGHT-ARM FAST-MEDIUM

Born: Leeds, Yorkshire, 29 August 1926

*Portrait of Dennis Good.*

First-class matches for Worcestershire: 1 versus Combined Services, New Road, Worcester, 31 July 1, 2 August 1946

Innings: 2; Not out: 1; Runs: 7; Highest score: 6 not out; Caught: 0; Wickets: 1; Best bowling: 1-60

*Combined Services won by five wickets. Thanks to 107 by Don Kenyon and half-centuries from Mike Ainsworth (50 not out) and Reg Perks (51) – all of whom, ironically, played for Worcestershire – the visitors closed on 429 all out. Dennis Good's only wicket was that of Middlesex's John Dewes, whom he had lbw for 10. He went wicketless in the second innings.*

*Dismissed for 232, Worcestershire were 'held together', with half-centuries from Allan White (58) and Roly Jenkins (69 not out).*

*Good was one of Dick Pollard's four first-innings victims; the great Lancastrian went on to take over 1,100 first-class wickets.*

*Following on, Worcestershire were dismissed for 280, White top-scoring with 95, which left the Combined Services a target of 84 to win, which they achieved for the loss of five wickets.*

*John Collinson and Norman Bennett were also making their debuts for Worcestershire in this game and feature elsewhere in this publication.*

Educated at Denstone College (where he became captain of the first XI) Dennis Good first featured in the school side as a 14-year-old in June 1941, against King Edward's School, Birmingham. Out of Denstone's 234-3 declared, David Beardsmore scored 132 not out and Good weighed in with figures of 6-5 as King Edward's were dismissed for just 15 runs in reply.

His daughter Jennifer told me recently what a talented young player her father was. Rather frail now, he told her that: '*When I was a young boy my father told me that if I was to score 100 runs in one match he would give me £100. I achieved this when I was about 11 or 12 years old! I also recall, when I was about the same age, I set a cricket record getting nine wickets for four runs.*' Sadly, Good cannot recall the detail of this.

In May 1943 he enlisted as an Air Training Corps cadet in Doncaster, having previously been a member of the Royal Air Force Volunteer Reserve while at school. Hoping to become a pilot, he was called up to the RAF just as the War was ending, and played cricket for them from 1945 until the end of 1947. Continuing to show great skill at other sports, from 1946–1947 he captained one of the Yorkshire Union of Golf Clubs teams.

While stationed with the RAF in Hereford he was physical education instructor for the recruits, a testimony to his athleticism.

*Good, seated on the left with the RAF Station Cricket XI in 1947.*

Good continued to play Yorkshire League cricket as a professional and had an unsuccessful trial for Yorkshire. He did, however, impress the Worcestershire scouts, leading to his selection for the Combined Services game in 1946. From 1949 until 1952, he studied textiles at Leeds University from which he had won a sports scholarship; while there he played for the cricket, rugby and golf teams.

*Dennis Good in action.*

Glamorgan had also been keeping an eye on his progress and in May 1947 he was called up when the older and more experienced pairing of Peter Judge and Austin Matthews were injured. Known by his team-mates as 'Glamorgan's next Harold Larwood', he had the ability to bowl at express pace.

He made his debut against the touring South Africans at Cardiff Arms Park, bowling Alan Melville for 29 and finishing with 1-79 from 21 overs. During the tour, Melville scored 1,547 runs – including six centuries – resulting in him being named as one of Wisden's five cricketers of the year in 1948.

In the final two weeks of June, Good played two more Championship matches for Glamorgan, against Surrey and Derbyshire, claiming six further wickets in total. Shortly afterwards, he had to abandon hopes of playing full-time cricket as a ruptured Achilles tendon forced him to retire. In an email, his sister Avril commented: *'He was a super quick bowler, and the stresses of bowling must have taken their toll.'*

Towards the end of the year, he returned to live in Horsforth near Leeds, where he worked for Hield Brothers of Halifax in the textile-manufacturing business. At this time he was also a drummer in a jazz band called The Sunny Ray Quartet.

He married Frances Mary Hoggard (known as Mary) in 1951 and in January the following year was faced with the offer of work in Belfast or Montreal. He chose the latter and set sail from Liverpool to Canada on the RMS *Empress of France*. His wife followed once he was settled. Travelling first class, he headed for St John, New Brunswick before settling in Montreal, Quebec.

Initially, he lived at an YMCA hostel and enjoyed mingling with local sports stars whom he had met. By now he was working for the large textile manufacturer Cleyn and Tinker, before he set up his own textile-import business in the 1970s. He would design suits and then travel to South Korea, China, Colombia, Japan and Poland to get them manufactured, then ship them back to Canada.

He was a great all-round sportsman, playing rugby, snooker and tennis. He had a golf handicap of two, captained the Westmount Golf Club and represented Montreal in a match against Ottawa. In Quebec he set up and captained the Rosemère Tennis Club.

In June 1953 Good played cricket twice for Montreal, firstly against Ottawa at the Westmount Athletic Ground in Montreal. In a seven-wicket defeat he scored two runs and bowled his five overs for 15 runs. The following year he was offered a place in the Canada side on a 15-match tour of the UK; he declined as he did not want to leave his wife or his work.

At the time of writing Good was living in a care home in Oakville, Ontario and was Worcestershire's oldest surviving first-class cricketer.

# GOODREDS

## WILLIAM ARTHUR GOODREDS – RIGHT-HAND BAT, RIGHT-ARM FAST-MEDIUM

Born: Pensnett, near Dudley, Staffordshire, 3 November 1920
Died: Dudley, West Midlands, 9 February 2014

*Portrait of Bill Goodreds.*

First-class matches for Worcestershire: 1 versus Cambridge University, New Road, Worcester, 25, 26, 27 June 1952

Innings: 1; Not out: 1; Runs: 4; Highest score: 4 not out; Caught: 0; Wickets: 0; Best bowling: 0-21

*Cambridge University won by six wickets. Worcestershire were dismissed for 295, with half-centuries for George Dews (54) and Roly Jenkins (85). Bill Goodreds, batting at number 10, finished four not out. The students were dismissed for 185 (Mike Stevenson 53). Jenkins claimed 8-82 while Goodreds bowled eight overs for 27 runs.*

*With Worcestershire declaring their second innings on 262-6 (Harry Moule 57 and Bob Broadbent 88 not out), Cambridge were set a challenging 373 to win. Raman Subba Row (68) and David Sheppard, with a magnificent 239 not out, ensured a six-wicket win for the visitors. Goodreds bowled just four overs for 21 runs. Harry Moule was also making his debut for Worcestershire in this game and features elsewhere in this publication.*

Having studied at the Sir Gilbert Claughton Grammar School in Dudley, Goodreds trained as a draughtsman and spent most of his professional life working for Henry Hope and Sons, a large metal manufacturer in Smethwick in the West Midlands.

His association with Worcestershire began in June 1939, in a second XI fixture against Warwickshire seconds at New Road. In Warwickshire's first innings Goodreds took 6-109 from 23 overs, including the key wicket of opener Norman Shortland for 110. It was a sound debut performance but the game ended in a draw.

During the War Goodreds served as a 'craftsman' with the Royal Electrical and Mechanical Engineers and in 1940 was evacuated from Dunkirk as part of Operation Dynamo. He later served under Field Marshal Montgomery with the Eighth Army during the North African and Italian campaigns.

He saw action at El-Alamein and Tobruk where he was part of the vehicle recovery and repair unit. Goodreds's son, John, told me a story about his father's Army career: *'He went in a private and came out a private! He did rise to the heady rank of lance corporal but lost his stripes due to some misdemeanour in Italy. I think he was caught using a military vehicle without permission to transport some of his Army mates around.'* He was discharged from the Army in 1945.

*Goodreds during the War, second from the right.*

On the resumption of cricket, Goodreds forged a name for himself as a fine Birmingham League cricketer with Dudley, a club he was to serve with great distinction for over 20 years.

In 1945 Goodreds married Winifred Nutting. They had two sons, John, born in 1947 and David, born in 1949. John continued the cricketing tradition, representing Worcestershire over-50s, -60s and -70s.

On 5 June 1948 Goodreds took a hat-trick in the Birmingham League game versus Walsall at Dudley and finished with figures of 5-30. He was presented with the match ball which he donated to the Worcestershire CCC heritage collection some years ago. It is now on display at the New Road ground.

Dudley CC's finest moment came in 1952 when they were crowned Birmingham and District League Champions. Their side included the great 'Black Bradman', George Headley. Goodreds commented that he always liked the picture below as it included the

Championship pennant. His generous spirit was further evidenced when he donated his winners' tankard to the Worcestershire CCC heritage collection.

*Dudley CC 1952. Goodreds is seated third from the left.*
*George Headley is seated, third from the right.*

Two years later, on 25 July 1954, Goodreds, a fiercely proud Black Countryman, had the honour to captain the Birmingham District XI against a West Indian XI in a game at Dudley in aid of George Headley's benefit. Included in the West Indies side were Everton Weekes and Clyde Walcott. Weekes scored 72 not out, out of a total of 161-6 declared.

Worcestershire's Hartley Lobban (known as Ken Lobban, who was also a professional boxer) was also in the West Indies side, while Worcestershire stalwarts Norman Whiting and Peter Jackson represented the District XI. Whiting scored 45; the innings closed on 134-2.

Goodreds's career with Dudley continued into the late-1950s. Included in this team picture are a young Ron Headley and Reg

Perks. Over a 16-year period Headley scored more than 20,000 runs for Worcestershire – and developed a reputation as an outstanding close catcher – while over a 25-year period Perks took in excess of 2,000 wickets for Worcestershire and remains the only bowler to reach that landmark for the Club.

*Dudley CC in the late-1950s. Goodreds is standing third from the right, Ron Headley is standing on the left and Reg Perks is seated, second from the right. On the back row (extreme right) is Ken Burns, who refereed the 1973 FA Cup final between Sunderland and Leeds United.*

In 1959, Goodreds moved to Wall Heath in the West Midlands, a house he shared with Winifred until she died in 1997 and in which he remained until he died at Russell's Hall Hospital, Dudley, in 2014.

In his later life, he had excelled at ten-pin bowling and well into his 80s continued to enjoy both ballroom dancing and his involvement as chairman of the Wolverhampton Area for the Institute of Advanced Motorists.

# GRISEWOOD

## FREDERICK HENRY GRISEWOOD – RIGHT-HAND BAT

Born: Daylesford, Worcestershire, 11 April 1888
Died: Grayshott, Hampshire, 15 November 1972

*Portrait of Freddy Grisewood.*

First-class matches for Worcestershire: 1 versus Oxford University, The Parks, Oxford, 11, 12, 13 June 1908

Innings: 2; Not out: 1; Runs: 7; Highest score: 6 not out; Caught: 0; Did not bowl

*Worcestershire won by 332 runs. In the first innings they were indebted to George Simpson-Hayward who, out of a total of 185, scored 105 in just 80 minutes.*

*Batting at number nine, Grisewood contributed a single before being caught by Roy Robinson (later becoming First Baron Robinson) off the bowling of Humphrey Gilbert who finished with 5-54. Gilbert went on to play 72 matches for Worcestershire between 1921 and 1930.*

*Simpson-Hayward continued his excellent form and took 6-13 in the University's first innings of 85. Batting for a second time, Worcestershire scored 362, William Burns striking 146 (in just over two hours at the crease). On this occasion, Grisewood finished, six not out, with Gilbert taking 6-170. Leaving Oxford 463 to win, all-rounder Ted Arnold made light work of their second innings claiming 7-51 as Oxford were dismissed for 130.*

*Guy Pawson, John Winnington and Eric Brownell were also making their debuts for Worcestershire in this game and feature elsewhere in this publication.*

Freddy Grisewood was born at Daylesford Rectory. His father, Arthur, was the local rector and his mother Lilian ran the family home. She was a gifted singer which had a huge influence on her son, helping shape his lifelong love of music. It was here that he spent an idyllic childhood, enjoying the countryside and developing a love of ball games, especially cricket, hockey (ultimately playing for Oxfordshire) and lawn tennis. He formed a strong doubles partnership with his brother and competed at many local tournaments. His other loves were fishing and shooting.

He attended prep school in Malvern Wells and then Radley College, where he captained the first XI cricket team in 1906. Shortly before leaving school, Grisewood made the late decision to join the Navy; however, he failed the examination to attend the Britannia Royal Naval College in Dartmouth and decided to continue with his academic studies, with the intention of joining the church. In preparation for reading classics at university, he sought support from a family friend, Canon Cyril Houghton of Blockley in Worcestershire, who coached him in readiness for the 'Smalls' university entrance examination. In 1907, Grisewood 'went up' to Magdalen College, Oxford, where he read classics, graduating in 1910.

Grisewood was a member of the Magdalen College hockey team which won the Inter-College Cup in the 1907–08 season and while he did not win a Blue he played in the University Freshman's match in 1908, representing E.L. Wright's XI against C.S. Hurst's XI. His team-mates included Frederick Burr and Guy Pawson, both of whom appear elsewhere in this publication.

*Magdalen College hockey team, 1907–08.*
*Grisewood is standing, extreme right.*

During that time he continued to play cricket for his local village side, Blockley and the University Authentics Cricket Club. Under the guidance of his friend and mentor, the composer and music historian Sir Hubert Parry, Grisewood's flair and aptitude for music and the theatre grew. He featured regularly in productions staged by the University drama society which toured many of the country's public schools.

By 1911 Grisewood was living in Earl's Court and pursuing a career away from the church. He trained for the music profession, which included time spent in Paris and Munich. His progress, however, was interrupted by the War.

On the day War was declared, Grisewood was playing in a tennis tournament in Lincolnshire against an old Cambridge Blue. On hearing the news they immediately agreed that the game should be 'scratched' and went their separate ways to join up. Grisewood joined his brother in the Oxfordshire and Buckinghamshire Light Infantry and the following month he received his commission as a second lieutenant. In March 1915 he married Betty Roffy, but they were divorced some years later.

Immediately after his wedding, Grisewood was posted to France where he encountered fierce fighting at Ploegsteert Wood in Flanders. He was taken ill with suspected trench fever and typhoid and convalesced at Sir Edward and Lady Michelham's home on The Riviera before returning to Osborne on the Isle of Wight for further treatment. Invalided out of the Army, he went to run the estate of the politician Charles Baring Young in Daylesford.

Following the birth of his daughter, Anne, in 1921, Grisewood turned his attention to giving singing and music lessons in order to supplement his income. Triggered by the death of his employer and with a young family to support, he decided that it was time for a career change. Good fortune was to follow when, after a speculative letter to a friend at the BBC, he was offered a 'test' as an announcer in July 1929 which he duly passed.

Grisewood's big break came in 1931 when he was asked to read the news, which necessitated moving from the Savoy Hill studio to Broadcasting House. Becoming an increasingly popular figure – made more famous by his inclusion as one of Wills's Cigarette cards radio celebrities – he had even become known as 'Uncle Freddy' to Children's Hour Listeners. Further evidence that his stock was rising came in May 1937 when he commentated on the first live outside television broadcast, the Coronation of King George VI.

In his 1952 autobiography, *The World Goes By*, he described the occasion: '*The BBC had only taken delivery of its first outside broadcast unit, which consisted of several vans, two days before the Coronation. Despite no one having any experience of operating the unit, it was placed at the top of Constitution Hill to catch the Royal Carriage as it went past. A message was sent to the King asking him to give a special wave for the camera but just as the Royal Carriage appeared in the distance, all the equipment failed. The engineer in charge swore, gave it a hefty kick and it all came to life again so the day was saved.*'

A month after the Coronation, Grisewood commentated on the first outside broadcast at Wimbledon and in 1938 hosted the first televised game show, called *Spelling Bee*.

On 8 March 1941 he married Aileen Scriven, who shared a common love of lawn tennis. Her sister was Peggy Scriven, the tennis player who was the first English woman to win the French Championships, in both 1933 and 1934, and who, in August 1933, was part of the losing British team in the Wightman Cup held at Forest Hills in New York.

During the War he continued to broadcast and support the War effort by presenting programmes such as '*On the Kitchen Front*', an initiative to keep the country fed. Such was the success that he was asked to support 'dig for victory' weeks which took the form of a series of talks at various locations around the country.

In 1948 Grisewood became the host and question master of the immensely popular *Any Questions* programme, which he hosted for 20 years. Such was his contribution to broadcasting that he was awarded the Officer of the Most Excellent Order of the British Empire, an OBE, in 1959.

*Grisewood and his wife collecting his OBE in 1959.*
*With them is their nephew Nicholas Vivian.*

# HALL

## BRIAN CHARLES HALL – RIGHT-HAND BAT, RIGHT-ARM MEDIUM

Born: Marylebone, London, 2 March 1934

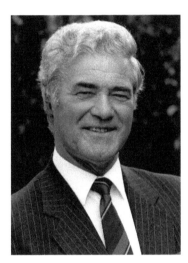

*Portrait of Brian Hall.*

First-class matches for Worcestershire: 3
- Versus Oxford University, New Road, Worcester, 30 June 2, 3 July 1956
- Versus Oxford University, The Parks, Oxford, 5, 6, 7 June 1957
- Versus Combined Services, New Road, Worcester, 19, 20, 21 June 1957

Innings: 4; Not out: 1; Runs: 34; Highest score: 21; Caught: 1; Wickets: 3; Best bowling: 2-11

*Against Oxford University #1. Worcestershire won by 131 runs. Peter Richardson (58) and George Dews (94) helped Worcestershire to 294 all out, Hall's contribution was 21. The students declared on 252-9 with Hall taking the wicket of Jimmy*

*Allan for four and holding a catch to dismiss M.J.K. Smith off Laddie Outschoorn for 49.*

*Declaring on 184-5 (Dews 62), Worcestershire set the visitors 227 to win. They were bowled out for 95 with Hall claiming the wickets of Allan and Peter Delisle.*

*John Chadd was making his first-class debut in this game and features elsewhere in this publication.*

*Against Oxford University #2. Worcestershire won by 178 runs. Declaring on 288-7 (Peter Richardson 76), Worcestershire dismissed Oxford for 188 with Len Coldwell taking 6-30. Hall went wicketless. In the second innings, 119 from Don Kenyon and 58 from 'Dick' Richardson allowed for a declaration at 207-5. Requiring 308 for victory, Oxford were dismissed for 129 with Coldwell claiming 5-18 and Hall going wicketless once more.*

*Against Combined Services, Worcestershire won by nine wickets. Combined Services were dismissed for 224 (Roly Jenkins, 7-98) with Hall bowling his six overs for 14 runs. Worcestershire were all out for 216 (Don Kenyon 61 and 'Dick' Richardson 50) with Hall falling for a duck to a catch by Raman Subba Row off Barry Knight.*

*Len Coldwell with 5-20 helped to dismiss the Combined Services for 88 with Worcestershire reaching their target of 97 (Kenyon 54 not out) for the loss of one wicket.*

Playing cricket as a junior for Stanmore CC, aged just 15, Hall went to Lord's for a trial to join the MCC ground staff. He was offered a place with them; however, his father would not allow him to leave school that year (1949). He was studying at Gregg's Commercial College at the time.

In 1950 MCC approached Hall once more and on this occasion his father relented and he started life as a professional cricketer earning £2-10s-0d per week. In a conversation I had with Hall he recalled: '*On my first morning I met a 15-year-old boy called John Murray (J.T. Murray, Middlesex and England wicket-keeper) and we became lifelong friends until he passed away in 2018. My job was selling scorecards but I also received nominal amounts of cash for bowling to MCC members in the nets. I'd also bowl to Gubby Allen and Walter Robins and they would pay 5s for the privilege and on match days I would operate the scoreboard and help with pitch-rolling prior to Test matches.*'

Hall also recalled that the West Indies toured England that year and saw them beat England for the first time ever in England, at Lord's.

In 1951 he progressed to what was known as the A staff, playing cricket for MCC in 'out matches' and bowling with and against the touring sides at Lord's. He started the 1952 season at Lord's and in June was called up for national service, where he spent two years playing for the Royal Artillery, the Army and an abundance of other Army cricket sides.

On leave from the forces in 1953, he had the privilege of bowling to the Australians in the nets at Lord's. Having faced Hall, Keith Miller took him to one side and asked if he could have a word. Asking him to compare the actions of Ron Archer and Ray Lindwall, he helped Hall identify that Lindwall's follow-though and sweep of the arm allowed him to generate more pace than Archer. As a result, Hall introduced this into his game.

Early in 1954 he returned to Lord's to play for MCC and Middlesex second XI, featuring alongside players such as John Murray and Eric Russell. It was during that spell that Maurice Jewell from Worcestershire went to Lord's looking for a seam bowler. Hall was selected from a group of five such bowlers and offered a contract with Worcestershire for 1955. Middlesex, however, would not release him and he signed a further one-year deal and remained with them. Worcestershire contacted Middlesex again at the end of 1955 and on this occasion they released him, so life started with his new county.

Hall made his Worcestershire second XI debut on 7 May 1956 against Warwickshire at Edgbaston. Later that month he claimed 4-53 and 3-54 in the drawn game versus Glamorgan and against Gloucestershire reached his highest second XI score of 20 (batting at number 11) and taking 3-96 in the drawn game.

He continued to show promise with returns of 4-80 in the return fixture with Warwickshire and 3-60 against Somerset. Playing 10 further games in 1957, Hall's best figures were 4-78 and 3-58 against Warwickshire. He also made regular appearances for the Club and Ground XI and in the game against City of Worcester Training College returned the figures of 5-10. In the following game he scored 52 not out in the 180-run victory over Worcester Royal Grammar School.

*Worcestershire CCC Club and Ground XI, 1957. Brian Hall is seated on the extreme right. Others who feature elsewhere in this publication are: John Chadd (front row, extreme left); Alf Tasker (standing, third from the left) and Ron Jones (standing, second from the right).*

Hall recalls this passage of his career with great affection. He told me that: *'I enjoyed only two seasons, 1956 and 1957, and played three times in the first XI. Appearances were limited in 1956 because it required a 'special registration' in order for me to play. There was only one registration available at the start of the season, which was awarded to Roy Booth because the incumbent 'keeper, Hugo Yarnold, had retired at the end of 1955 due to persistent knee injuries.*

*'However, in the second XI I bowled more than twice as many overs (290 in 1956 and 240 in 1957) than the next highest bowler and took a total of 72 wickets, which amounted to more than 40 more than any other bowler.'*

At the end of the 1957 season Hall married Brenda Jones, just one week after being best man at John Chadd's wedding. He rejoined Stanmore CC where he had been a junior member prior to joining the MCC staff in 1950.

He also started to work for Phillips Records in the sales office and quickly progressed to sales representative and on to area manager, controlling a six-strong sales team. Ten years after entering the record industry he teamed up with Larry Page as marketing director and they formed Penny Farthing Records, gaining international experience of the record industry.

Four years later he joined a major American record company, RCA, as sales manager, controlling a sales force of 24 people. He became the UK's marketing manager and later European marketing manager, which entailed a lot of travel in both Europe and America. Hall worked closely with many artists such as David Bowie, Dolly Parton, Perry Como and Julian Bream. Getting older, however, and wanting more time at home, he joined a plastics manufacturing company, Lin Pac Group, for which he was managing director for the last 15 years of his working life.

Hall continued his involvement in cricket and studied at Lilleshall where he attained the 'A' level Cricket Coaching Certificate. During his studies he shared a room with Sussex's Jim

Parks and undertook some coaching for MCC in the winter nets back at Lord's.

In 1959 Hall re-joined Stanmore CC yet again and subsequently played in the first team for 23 years, taking 1,700 wickets in all games and captaining the side from 1966 until 1972. He has served Stanmore as chairman and since 1996 has been the longest-serving president in the Club's 160-year history, an achievement he is particularly proud of.

In 1969 Hall became a member of MCC and was invited to play 'one more' game of cricket and represent the MCC team against Scotland and the Netherlands. He declined the invitation as his first commitment was to Stanmore CC.

Hall's affinity with Worcestershire has never dwindled. He has always been a keen member of Worcestershire CCC's old players' association and without fail attends its annual reunion. He has been retired now for 23 years; however, he remains active and has been elected president of Northwood Golf Club for the next three years.

*Worcestershire's old players' reunion, 2010. Hall is standing (seventh from the left) in the centre at the back wearing a dark green blazer. John Chadd is seated, third from the right.*

As recently as December 2019, in conjunction with Neil Robertson the curator of the MCC Collection, Hall recorded an hour-long interview at Lord's describing what it was like being on the ground staff in the 1950s. He's thrilled that his reminiscences will be added to the MCC archives and that others will get the opportunity to share the enjoyment of his life in cricket.

# HUSSAIN

## MEHRIYAR HUSSAIN – RIGHT-HAND BAT, OFF-BREAK BOWLER

Born: South Shields, County Durham, 17 October 1963

*Portrait of Mel Hussain.*

First-class matches for Worcestershire: 1 versus Cambridge University, Fenner's, Cambridge, 12, 13, 14 June 1985

Innings: 1; Not out: 0; Runs: 4; Highest score: 4; Caught: 0; Did not bowl

*Match drawn. While Worcestershire entertained Zimbabwe at New Road, seven players were given first-class debuts in the match at Cambridge. Three of them – Lawrence Smith, Stuart Lampitt and Paul Bent all subsequently played Championship cricket. Four of them – Mel Hussain, along with Harshad Patel, Brian Barrett and Mike Scothern, who feature elsewhere in this publication, were not afforded the same opportunity.*

*Thanks to half-centuries from acting captain and wicket-keeper, David Humphries (62 not out) and David Banks (50 not out) a crisis was averted and Worcestershire posted 216-5 declared. Hussain scored four in his only innings for the County. Due to bad weather the University's reply was restricted to 143-6.*

Mehriyar (Mel) Hussain is the brother of the former England captain Nasser Hussain. Despite being born in the UK, he lived the early part of his life in Chennai. India, where his father Jawad

(Joe) Hussain played a first-class game for Madras CC. In 1975 the family settled in Essex and four years later Hussain continued his education at Forest School, Snaresbrook near Walthamstow, while his father established and ran an indoor cricket school in Ilford. The club at Ilford is where his senior league career began, a team he was ultimately to captain.

During his time at Ilford, he caught the eye of Don Wilson who was MCC's chief coach. By 1981 he had joined the staff of MCC Young Cricketers, an intake which included Dermot Reeve, Martin Crowe and Worcestershire's Damian D'Oliveira. The highlight of his career to this point came when he played in a Select XI at Lord's against a multi-national side including Pakistan captain Mushtaq Mohammad and Hampshire batsman Nick Pocock. In a five-wicket win, he dismissed both players with his off-spin and was subsequently given a trial by Hampshire.

He commented on his Young Cricketers' experience saying: *'Lord's was my home. I could walk around wearing my spikes in the Long Room and it was a wonderful time. All the same, I was still an Essex boy, and although I was playing some second XI cricket for them they couldn't offer me a contract. They sent me their blessings and told me to play as much cricket as I could, hence the trial at Hampshire.'*

While representing Hythe and Dibden in the Southern League, Hussain duly played for Hampshire seconds from 1982 until 1984. In May 1984 he scored 79 not out and 55 not out in an eight-wicket victory over Somerset, and in August reached his highest second XI score when he was run out for 95 against Sussex at Southampton. He was offered a two-year contract at Hampshire; however, with their wealth of talent, a first-team appearance eluded him. Essex heard about this and made a counter offer which he admits, in hindsight, he should have accepted but did not.

Hussain played two games for Warwickshire seconds at the start of 1985, was offered a contract by them but decided instead to pursue a career with Credit Suisse in the City and at a later date J.P. Morgan. Having turned down the Warwickshire contract he transferred allegiance to Worcestershire and after just one second-team game in June he played in his only first-class game against Cambridge University. This was followed by two more second XI games. In total, he scored 106 runs in five innings with a top score of 42 versus Somerset at Kidderminster.

For the 1986 season Hussain returned to Essex and continued to play second XI matches; however, his cricketing career at league and amateur level was entering a new phase. With Wanstead he won the national indoor competition and played for Fives and Heronians for 10 years, twice winning the Essex League title, another national indoor title and the European indoor title in Vienna. He also made 50 in the defeat to Teddington in the inaugural Evening Standard Knockout Final at The Oval.

Between 1991 and 1994 Hussain played 20 games for England, including matches against the Australian and New Zealand tourists. In 1994 he was in the victorious team that beat Worcestershire's Club and Ground XI by 10 wickets at New Road. He did not bat but caught Vikram Solanki off the bowling of Richard Ellwood for 30.

A move to Gidea Park and Romford followed and he captained them to League success in his first season. This was followed with a 10-year stint playing for High Riding in the Mid Essex League.

In November 2010 he moved from Credit Agricole to UBS (Union Bank of Switzerland) as executive director of their hedge fund sales desk and continued to play his cricket despite the added pressures of working in the City.

By 2014, having qualified to play over-50s cricket, Hussain travelled with England to Australia for the over-50s World Cup in 2017–2018, scoring 56 in England's semi-final defeat to Pakistan. He went on to make eight appearances in the competition.

*Hussain representing England over-50s in South Africa, 2020.*

By now, Hussain had scored a hundred 100s at club level, yet his appetite to continue playing was greater than ever. More success followed in 2019 when he captained Essex over-50s to victory in the competition final against Yorkshire, a success made all the sweeter because his side had failed to secure the title on several previous occasions.

In March 2020 he played in his second World Cup event, and in March just prior to lockdown in South Africa the game he played against Namibia was the only cricket to be played anywhere in the world at that time.

His son Reece played first-class cricket for Oxford MCCU against Surrey and now plays for Hertfordshire and in 2015 Hussain followed his son to Bishop's Stortford CC to play Premier League cricket.

In 2020 Mel Hussain was inducted into the *Wisden Cricket Monthly* Club Cricket Hall of Fame where he was described as: '*a titan of club cricket with a famous name and a sensational record*'.

Summing up the highlights of his career it's fitting that the final words go to the player himself: '*My fondest memories are more after life as a professional and playing league cricket. Touring with the Cricket Club Conference (between 2000 and 2015) to* places like Barbados, Denmark and Dubai, plus my selection for the England Amateur XI to play against Australia, Pakistan, New Zealand and Sri Lanka.

Hussain playing for Essex over-50s.

'Domestically, I think the highlights have to be the two Premier League double-hundreds and I have also joined the 100 league-hundreds club. On my long journey I have won nine League titles, two Twenty-20 titles and seven indoor League titles including the nationals and European indoor title. So, as I say, cricket has been my life and my enthusiasm has never wavered.'

# ISAAC

## HERBERT WHITMORE ISAAC – RIGHT-HAND BAT

Born: Hallow, Worcester, 11 December 1899
Died: Fig Tree Farm, Chisekesi, Zambia, 26 April 1962

*Herbert Isaac during his debut game in 1919.*

First-class matches for Worcestershire: 3
  - Versus Warwickshire, Edgbaston, Birmingham, 4 and 5 August 1919
  - Versus H K Foster's XI, New Road, Worcester, 15 and 16 August 1919
  - Versus Warwickshire, New Road Worcester, 25 and 26 August 1919

Innings: 3; Not out: 0; Runs: 32; Highest score: 23; Caught: 0; Wickets: 0; Best bowling: 0-10

*Against Warwickshire #1, match drawn. Winning the toss and batting, Worcestershire were bowled out for 330 with Wing*

113

Commander Shakespeare (62) and 'Dick' Burrows (82) holding the innings together. Batting at number nine, Isaac's contribution was four before being bowled by Jack Smart.

Warwickshire replied with 391-9 declared, Horace Venn top-scoring with 151 before becoming one of Burrows' four wickets. Worcestershire replied with 162-0, with the not-out batsmen Alfred Cliff (81) and Shakespeare (67). Rupert Rogers was also making his debut for Worcestershire in this game and features elsewhere in this publication.

Against H.K. Foster's XI, match drawn. Worcestershire declared their first innings on 341-5, with Arthur Jewell top-scoring with 128. H.K. Foster's XI was dismissed for 203 with only Sidney Freeman (58) and John MacLean (59 not out) making contributions of note. MacLean went on to play 45 times for Worcestershire between 1922 and 1924, while Colonel Bill Taylor was the pick of the bowlers taking 5-56. Isaac bowled two overs for 10 runs.

Worcestershire declared their second innings on 183-7, with Isaac, opening the batting, run out for 23. Worcestershire set H.K. Foster's XI 322 to win; they closed on 182-4 with Frank Phillips scoring 59.

Against Warwickshire #2, match drawn. In a low-scoring game Worcestershire were all out for 187, Isaac scoring five and becoming one of Edward Hewetson's two victims. Harry Howell finished with 6-69. In reply Warwickshire were bowled out for 145 (Horace Venn 58) with Major Maurice Jewell taking 7-56.

Worcestershire declared their second innings on 102-7 (Isaac did not bat); setting the visitors 145 to win, they finished on 70-2.

At the turn of the last century, the influence of the Isaac family on Worcestershire cricket was immense. In 1865 the family agreed, with the newly formed Worcestershire County Cricket Club, that their home, Boughton Park, could be used to stage home fixtures. It remained the home of Worcestershire CCC until it moved to its New Road ground in preparation for its inaugural first-class fixture in 1899.

Herbert Isaac (known as Bunny) was the son of Arthur Isaac, a banker in the firm Berwick Ledmore and Company. They ultimately merged with Capital and Counties Bank and in due course were taken over by Lloyd's Bank. Arthur Isaac played 52 matches for Worcestershire between 1899 and 1911 and served as honorary club treasurer at the time of Paul Foley's tenure as secretary.

Arthur's younger brother, John, played four matches for Worcestershire in 1907. In addition to being a skilful cricketer he was a gifted horseman who, in 1911, won the Cairo Grand National on a horse he owned and trained. Tragically, both men were to lose their lives in World War One and are commemorated in the cloisters' windows in Worcester Cathedral.

Before Arthur's death the estate and house were leased to a Lancashire industrialist named Marriage; the Isaac family then moved to Bowbrook House near Pershore. The estate, which was then being managed by a trust on behalf of the surviving members of the Isaac family, was bought in 1927 by the Worcester City Golf Club of Tolladine and became the Worcester Golf and Country Club.

Like his father and uncle before him, in 1913, Herbert Isaac first attended Harrow School. While he didn't play in the annual cricket fixture against Eton at Lord's, he did play against them at Harrow-on-the-Hill in June 1917, scoring three and bowling three overs for 12 runs in a drawn game, which Eton 'won on first innings'.

At Harrow, he was a member of Rendalls House, where, in addition to playing cricket, he excelled at golf and rackets. In April

1918, the *Harrovian Magazine* reported a defeat in the final of the Rackets Challenge Competition and also reported that he was to be made a lance-corporal cadet at the Royal Military Academy at Sandhurst, where he was based form 1918 until 1919.

*Worcester Cathedral cloisters windows commemorating the lives of A.W. Isaac and J.E.V. Isaac.*

Having played three first-class games Isaac represented Worcestershire on one further occasion, a two-day friendly game against MCC at New Road.

*Worcestershire CCC in 1919 – H.W. Isaac, standing extreme right. Rupert Rogers, who appears elsewhere in this publication, is standing extreme left.*

In this fixture arranged by Lord Deerhust, in response to MCC's 277, Worcestershire could only muster 78 runs, Isaac contributing a single. The MCC side included John Walford,

Robert Berkeley and John Coventry, all of whom were to play for Worcestershire.

Isaac continued to play local cricket, captaining St John's Cricket Club in Worcester for whom he nearly scored a 100 centuries. It was reported that he was immensely popular among local cricketers, not just because of his prowess with the bat but because of his outstanding personality.

In December 1919, Isaac joined the 3rd Battalion of the Worcester Regiment where he served as a lieutenant before retiring in 1924. Isaac then embarked on a career in the Civil Service, working in Kenya. In July 1925 and October 1926 he played cricket for the 'Officials' against the 'Settlers' in Nairobi and made something of a name for himself on the golfing circuit. He won the Rift Valley Championship in 1928 and again in 1938–39 and was runner up in 1937. In 1931 he won the Plateau Golf Championship and with his partner G.R. Grimwood won the pairs tournament in 1938, lifting the Gooding Cup.

In June 1940, Isaac joined the Royal Air Force Volunteer Reserve as a pilot officer working in the administration department. The increased administrative demands of the RAF were met by the recruitment or appointment of retired officers, academics and qualified administrators, who were commissioned into a new branch named Admin and Special Duties. Remaining in North Africa he served at both of the RAF stations at Abu Sueir and Fayid in Egypt.

Following the War Isaac lived in Zambia, retiring to Fig Tree Farm where he remained until his death in 1962. He was survived by his wife Mary Beatrice.

# ISLES

## DEREK ISLES – RIGHT-HAND BAT, WICKET-KEEPER

Born: Bradford, West Yorkshire, 14 October 1943

*Portrait of Derek Isles.*

First-class matches for Worcestershire: 1 versus The Pakistanis, New Road, Worcester, 19, 21, 22 August 1967

Innings: 2; Not out: 2; Runs: 21; Highest score: 17 not out; Caught: 1; Stumped: 1

*Match drawn. The Pakistanis won the toss and batted and were indebted to Saeed Ahmed with 147 and Hanif Mohammad with 74. Basil D'Oliveira was the pick of the Worcestershire bowlers claiming 4-75, while Isles took his first catch to dismiss Ghulam Abbas off the bowling of Glenn Turner for 32.*

*Worcestershire were dismissed for 313 (Tom Graveney 99 and D'Oliveira 96), with Saeed Ahmed continuing his good all-round form with 5-38. Batting at number nine, Isles made a creditworthy 17 not out.*

*The tourists declared their second innings at 225-5 with Hanif Mohammad scoring 118, before the combination of Isles and Turner struck again, on this occasion Isles stumping the 'Little Master'.*

*Requiring 282 to win, Worcestershire closed on 142-6 with Ron Headley (68) and Isles (4) the not-out batsmen.*

Isles's lifelong love of cricket was nurtured at Lapage School in Bradford where one of his teachers, having spotted his talent, mentored him from an early age and helped shape his cricketing career. From the age of 16, Isles played in the Bradford League, the majority of the time playing as a professional, especially as teams were allowed four paid professionals at any one time.

In June 1962 he made the first of five appearances for Yorkshire second XI in the game against Durham at Dewsbury in a Minor Counties Championship fixture. Four dismissals did his reputation no harm, but the star of the show was Mike Fearnley (brother of Worcestershire's Duncan Fearnley, the world-renowned bat manufacturer), who took six wickets in each innings as Yorkshire won by eight wickets.

His final game for Yorkshire seconds was against Cheshire at the Ellerman Line Sports Club, Hoylake at the end of July. The Yorkshire side included well-known names such as Geoffrey Boycott, Brian Bolus, Chris Balderstone and Mike Smedley. Despite being run out for nought in the second innings, Isles had the satisfaction of stumping the great Glamorgan off-spinner Jim McConnon for 37 as the match was drawn.

In 1964 Isles played three second XI matches for Nottinghamshire and in July 1966 one further game for Somerset seconds. By the end of the month, however, he was playing for Worcestershire seconds and in 15 matches took 26 catches and 12 stumpings, enough to justify his selection as cover for Roy Booth, who was being rested for the Pakistan game.

*Don Kenyon (on the left), Derek Isles and Glenn Turner in 1967.*

*Berrow's Worcester Journal* reported that: 'Today, Don Kenyon began his last match at New Road before he retires after 22 years of first-class cricket with Worcestershire, nine as captain and he is seen wishing good luck to Glenn Turner (right) and Derek Isles who are making their debuts in the game. Derek Isles may be specially registered for Championship matches this year.'

I asked Isles about his recollections of the game: '*When I initially went for trials Gilbert Parkhouse was coach; however, just as I was offered a contract he departed and I was left to my own devices. I must have done OK, though, to merit selection for this game. I remember fondly playing football practice sessions with Len Coldwell and Jack Flavell after which the secretary, Joe Lister, poked his head around the dressing room door and told me and Glenn that we were playing. The day of the game was the first time I met Don Kenyon. I knew of him by reputation as a hard, attacking captain.*

'*I remember Glenn very well. I played a lot with him in the seconds. He stood next to me at slip in our debut game with the captain in the gully. Glenn was a part-time bowler and after he*

*[Hanif Mohammad] reached his hundred, he waltzed down the pitch and I stumped him ... not a bad victim to get, really.'*

Isles's final appearance in second XI cricket was for Hampshire seconds in a game against Glamorgan at Northlands Road, Southampton in September 1968. In a four-wicket victory he signed off with a catch and a stumping to conclude this element of his cricketing career.

By trade Isles worked in the laundry business and did so for over 50 years. He was operations director for over 18 years with a national company before moving to a family-owned company to become the managing director for the next 14 years. His next move was to a publicly listed company where, once more, he was appointed managing director for 15 years.

During this time he continued to play Bradford League cricket, with some success. He played for Queensbury, Undercliffe, Bingley and Keighley, frequently winning the award for best wicket-keeper on the circuit.

*Bingley CC made history in 1969 by winning the Bradford League Championship and Priestley Cup double. Isles is on the front row, second from the left.*

Keighley CC was Isles's last club in Bradford League cricket, where again he won the local newspaper's best wicket-keeper award. He left the Club when his job took him to Scotland where he played major league standard for Clydesdale Cricket Club in west Scotland. They won the League and both cups.

*Keighley CC in 1977. Isles is on the back row, extreme left.*

In 2008, having been in the laundry business all his professional life, Isles was nominated and accepted as a member of the Worshipful Company of Launderers. Having joined the Company he became eligible to become a freeman of the City of London which was granted to him in the same year.

Isles moved to Louth in Lincolnshire in 2015. He has been married to Elayne for over 55 years and serves as vice-chairman and trustee director of Lindsey Citizens' Advice Service, a volunteering role providing support with issues affecting people's lives.

# JACKSON

## JOHN FREDERICK CECIL JACKSON – RIGHT-HAND BAT, RIGHT-ARM MEDIUM

Born: Meopham, Kent, 8 May 1880
Died: Kidderminster, Worcestershire, 22 November 1968

*Frederick Jackson in his school days.*

First-class matches for Worcestershire: 1 versus Oxford University, The Parks, Oxford, 23, 24, 25 May 1907

Innings: 2; Not out: 0; Runs: 6; Highest score: 6; Caught: 0; Did not bowl

*Oxford University won by 86 runs. Batting first, Oxford were dismissed for 120 with Ted Arnold taking 5-38. For Oxford, Clarence Bruce – the gifted sportsman who excelled at golf, lawn tennis, rackets and cricket – carried his bat for 64.*

*In reply Worcestershire were bowled out for 155, John Lowe taking 6-43 including the wicket of Jackson who was caught without score. The students were then bowled out for 241, the mainstay of the innings being G.N. Foster (who played 81 matches for Worcestershire between 1903 and 1914) who scored 88 before he became one of Arnold's five second-innings victims.*

*Requiring 207 to win, Worcestershire were all out for 120 with three wickets apiece for Humphrey Gilbert (who played 72 matches for Worcestershire between 1921 and 1939), Lowe and George Molineux. Jackson's contribution was six before being run out. Norman Jolly was also making his debut for Worcestershire in the game and features elsewhere in this publication.*

Frederick Jackson was the youngest of six children. His father, Captain John Boddington Jackson, was born in Africa and began his career as a soldier there, before returning to England in 1861 to live in Kent.

Educated at Tonbridge School, Jackson played for the cricket first XI and the rugby XV.

*Tonbridge rugby XV in 1896 –*
*Jackson is standing at the back in the centre.*

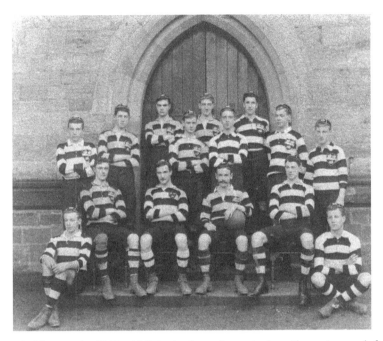

*Tonbridge rugby XV in 1897 – Jackson is seated on the extreme left.*

In April 1899 Jackson made his first appearance in Birmingham League cricket for Dudley and played for them on 16 occasions that season. Playing against Kidderminster in August he top-scored with 57 as Dudley lost by 107 runs, thanks to 119 not out from Stanley Gethin who was to play four matches for Worcestershire between 1900 and 1901.

Saving his best until the end of the season, Jackson starred in the match against Aston Unity on 26 August. He top-scored with 70 out of a total of 163 all out, but in reply Aston Unity were dismissed for just 84 as Jackson claimed 7-45 from 13 overs. The match report stated that: *'Aston Unity's E.H. Durban, who made 27, was the only succeeding batsman who could do anything with Jackson's bowling.'*

Two years later, on 5 March 1901, Jackson made the newspaper headlines once more, but for the wrong reason. He was summoned by Tonbridge Angling Club and Fish Preservation Society for illegal fishing in the Medway. He pleaded guilty but did so in the belief that his father always applied for a family licence. No such licence had been applied for. He duly paid the £1,8s and 6d fine.

By 1906, Jackson was playing for Worcestershire second XI. In the game against Warwickshire at Edgbaston in August in Worcestershire's second innings, he top-scored with 76 as they came close to reaching the unlikely target of 388 to win, closing on 343-7.

The same year Jackson invested in The Diamond Brewery at Kate's Hill, near Dudley in the West Midlands. Initially, Joseph Plant had brewed on the site up until 1899 and in the same year the Diamond Brewery Company Ltd was registered, but two years later it went bankrupt. The Five Quarter Brewery and the Brewery Tap (an off licence), together with The Black Horse and The Loving Lamb pubs, were sold at auction to William Hutchings and Frederick Jackson.

*Jackson's Brewery.*

On 31 December 1906 the partnership between Hutchings and Jackson was dissolved and the brewery then traded as J.F.C. Jackson. In 1916 the concern became J.F.C. Jackson Ltd and the business continued until June 1937, when it was bought by Darby's Brewery Ltd of Greets Green, West Bromwich along with 15 pubs.

*The J.F.C. Jackson Brewery, Kate's Hill, Dudley.*

In 1907, Jackson made his Minor Counties Championship debut playing for Worcestershire second XI in the fixture against Surrey second XI at the War Memorial Ground, Amblecote, in Stourbridge. In an innings and 132-run defeat, opening the batting he top-scored 37 as Worcestershire were dismissed in their second innings for 104.

On 22 June 1909, at St Mary's Church in Kidderminster, Jackson married Mary Constance Goodwin. They were to have two children, a daughter, Edith Mary, known as Molly, and a son, Jack.

Joining the Army in 1914, Jackson served as a lieutenant with 365 Company of the Army Service Corps which had been formed in May 1915. The Army Service Corps Mechanical Transport Depot Companies filled a variety of administrative, recruitment, training and re-supply roles. While the base depots were usually in the United Kingdom, the advanced depots – of which Jackson was part – were located further up the lines of communication. Jackson was based in Abbeville in France with the Second Advanced Mechanical Depot and later in Cologne with the Military Transport Depot serving with the British Army of the Rhine. He subsequently left the Army in 1922.

The census for 1939 shows that Jackson had retired. However, during World War Two he served in the 10th Stourbridge Battalion of the Home Guard. He was commissioned as a lieutenant on 1 August 1942 and served in that capacity until 1944.

*10th Battalion Worcestershire Home Guard in 1940.*

After the War he continued to live at Springbrook House, Blakedown, near Kidderminster, until he died in 1968, leaving an estate valued at. £75,283.

# JOLLY

## NORMAN WILLIAM JOLLY – WICKET-KEEPER AND BATSMAN

Born: Mintaro, Adelaide, South Australia, 5 August 1882
Died: Adelaide, South Australia, 18 May 1954

*Portrait of Norman Jolly.*

First-class matches for Worcestershire: 1 versus Oxford University, The Parks, Oxford, 23, 24, 25 May 1907

Innings: 2; Not out: 1; Runs: 9; Highest score: 8; Caught: 3; Stumped: 0; Did not bowl

*Oxford University won by 86 runs. Batting first, Oxford were dismissed for 120 with Ted Arnold taking 5-38, including the wicket of Oxford's captain, Egerton Wright, who was caught behind by Jolly for two. Clarence Bruce, a gifted sportsman who excelled at golf, lawn tennis, rackets and cricket, carried his bat for 64.*

*In reply, Worcestershire were bowled out for 155, John Lowe taking 6-43 while Humphrey Gilbert (who played 72 matches for Worcestershire between 1921 and 1939) claimed three wickets*

*including that of Jolly for eight. The students were then bowled out for 241, with Jolly taking two more catches behind the stumps. The mainstay of the innings was G.N. Foster (who played 81 matches for Worcestershire between 1903 and 1914), who scored 88 before he became one of Arnold's five second-innings victims.*

*Requiring 207 to win, Worcestershire were all out for 120 with three wickets apiece for Gilbert, Lowe and George Molineux. Jolly finished the innings one not out. John Jackson was also making his debut for Worcestershire in the game and features elsewhere in this publication.*

Norman Jolly, one of eight children, was the son of a storekeeper, Henry Jolly and his wife Annie.

He was educated at Mintaro State School, Prince Alfred College and the University of Adelaide, where, in 1901, he obtained his BSc with first-class honours in physics and mathematics. He distinguished himself in sport, playing A-grade cricket, rowing in the University eight and representing South Australia in Australian rules football.

In December 1897 he played for Prince Albert's College in the annual cricket fixture against St Peter's College, Adelaide, scoring just the single run in a four-wicket defeat.

*South Australia state side in 1901. Jolly is on the back row fifth from the right wearing a striped shirt, flat cap and with his arms folded.*

Jolly played his club Australian rules for Norwood – known as 'The Redlegs' on account of the colour of their socks – representing them in 21 games between 1899 and 1900. He was considered one of the Club's leading players and was selected for South Australia in an interstate match against Victoria in 1901, before transferring across to the newly formed Sturt Football Club to play alongside his brother, Bertram.

After working as a schoolteacher in Queensland, in 1904, Jolly went to Balliol College, Oxford as South Australia's first Rhodes Scholar, a prestigious award. There he enjoyed playing cricket, rugby, golf and rowing in the College eight and in 1907 graduated as a bachelor of arts with a first in natural sciences. He continued to study under Sir William Schlich, and briefly in Europe, to obtain the Oxford diploma of forestry, and later that year joined the Indian Forest Service in Burma.

He left there believing that '*an Australian should do his job for his own country*' and in 1909 returned to teach at Geelong Church of England Grammar School. In 1910 he became an instructor in forestry for the South Australian Woods and Forests Department. There he established the first course in higher forestry training in Australia and in 1911 was also assistant conservator of forests.

On 18 August 1911 Jolly married a widow, Mary Clyatt Gellert, and shortly after moved to Queensland as director of forests. There he began the state's first silviculture research programme and, having reviewed the degrading and dwindling condition of the forests, implemented a sustained-yield policy, beginning his battle to retain land for forest use rather than exploitation and sale. One conclusion from his Queensland experience was the lack of trained foresters in Australia. He stated: '*I consider that the training of students for the State Forestry Department is a matter of very great importance. It is obvious that the forestry interests of all states will be most economically and efficiently served by the foundation of one central school for the whole of Australia.*'

Jolly remained in Queensland until 1918 when he became one of the forestry commissioners in New South Wales. An appointment as the first professor of forestry at the University of Adelaide followed in 1925; however, that school was closed by the Commonwealth Government in 1926 and it was transferred to Canberra where it became the Australian Forestry School. Jolly resigned to return to New South Wales as sole forestry commissioner.

After repeated conflicts with the government over policy, Jolly retired in October 1933 due to ill health, returned to Adelaide and in 1937 undertook consultancy work with New Zealand Perpetual Forests Ltd. In 1939 he became forestry consultant to the South Australian Woods and Forests Department and was appointed as a member of the South Australian Forestry Board. He was elected an honorary member of the Institute of Foresters of Australia in 1953.

Jolly's outstanding characteristic was his professional integrity. He commanded the utmost respect of students and colleagues alike and was equally recognised for his academic brilliance. He is credited with the establishment of proper forest management in Queensland. His 'Silvicultural notes on forest trees in Queensland' and 'The structure and identification of Queensland woods', published by the Public Lands Department in 1917, were pioneering technical forestry publications in the state.

Jolly died on 18 May 1954 and in the same year the Institute of Foresters of Australia honoured him with the establishment of the N.W. Jolly Medal as its highest award for services to forestry in Australia. As a memorial, in 1957 a cairn was erected in the Norman Jolly Memorial Grove in the Moonpar State Forest on the north coast of New South Wales.

Subsequently, a picnic area of old growth trees and logging relics was established to create the Norman Jolly Picnic Area in Nymboi-Binderay National Park near Dorrigo in New South Wales, a lasting tribute to a man who made such an impact in his field of work.

*The cairn at the Norm Jolly Memorial Grove.*

*The Norm Jolly Picnic Area.*

# JONES

## RONALD JONES – RIGHT-HAND BATSMAN

Born: Tettenhall, Wolverhampton, Staffordshire, 9 September 1938
Died: Dudley, Staffordshire, 30 April 2019

*Portrait of Ron Jones.*

First-class matches for Worcestershire: 1 versus Cambridge University, New Road, Worcester, 22, 23, 24 June 1955

Innings: 2; Not out: 0; Runs: 25; Highest score: 23; Caught: 0; Did not bowl

*Cambridge University won by an innings and 76 runs. Cambridge were dismissed for 262 with notable scores from Vincent Lumsden (99) and Swaranjit Singh (79 not out). Worcestershire's response was disastrous: they were bowled out for 47 in just 32 overs. Adding to his half-century, Singh took 6-20 from 13 overs including the wicket of Jones for two.*

*Following on, Worcestershire were bowled out for 139 with Singh taking 4-43 and Gamini Goonesena 6-49, to wrap up a*

*straightforward innings victory. Jones fared better in the second innings, batting at number six he top-scored with 23.*

Ron Jones's family ran a newsagent's business in Wordsley in the West Midlands, living initially in Wall Heath and later moving to Kingswinford. A Black Country man, Jones went to St Mary's School in Kingswinford and Brierley Hill Secondary Technical School. There, his prowess as a fine sportsman shone through, and he became a regular member of Brierley Hill Schoolboys Area football team.

His footballing talent was spotted by those at the highest level and he signed as an amateur to play for Wolverhampton Wanderers. Attending training one evening a week, he was reimbursed with expenses of 5s.

Jones appeared in the Wolves' Wolverhampton Amateur League team and became a regular in the Worcestershire Combination side. When he left Wolves he was given a ringing endorsement by the legendary manager Stan Cullis, who said: *'I hope you turn out to be as good a cricketer as you are a footballer.'* He continued to play local football for Lye Town and Stourbridge Football Club.

As a young boy, Jones's interest in cricket was kindled when he was a scorer for Himley Cricket Club. Later he made the transition to playing for them and in a match early in his career took 5-0 against Bewdley. He then moved to Stourbridge in the Birmingham League and, following prompting from his grandmother, replied to an advert in the *Sporting Star* to attend trials for Worcestershire. He recalled facing Derek Pearson *'at his very quickest'*, but did well enough to secure a contract. (Derek Pearson played 74 matches for Worcestershire from 1954 to 1961)

Jones had first played for Worcestershire Club and Ground XI in 1954, progressing to the second XI the following season.

*Worcestershire Club and Ground XI versus Prince Henry's Grammar
School at Evesham in 1954. Jones is seated front row, extreme right.*

In 1955 he batted 15 times, scoring 221 runs with a highest
score of 46 in the drawn game against Somerset, in early June at
The Bottoms Ground in Pershore. By now he was also building a
reputation as an outstanding cover-point fielder.

At the end of the month Jones made his first-class debut against
Cambridge University, becoming the County's third youngest
player (at 16 years, 286 days) to make his first-class debut. Mike
Passey (standing extreme left in the above picture), at 16 years and
63 days, is still Worcestershire's youngest first-class cricketer.

The Worcestershire CCC yearbook for 1956, however, did not
provide a glowing report on the game: '*The sooner Worcestershire
forget the game, the better! Their first innings was the lowest
score they ever made against either University and the recognised
batsmen did no better in the second innings. Lumsden repeated his
success of 1954 – he scored 93 and 107 – and Singh had a grand
match as an all-rounder as did Goonesena, but their bowling was
flattered.*'

At the end of his third season, cutbacks meant that Jones was
one of several young players who were released. Despite being

encouraged by Peter Richardson to try his luck at Kent, and Jock Livingston at Northants, Jones decided to return to play for Stourbridge and continue to work locally.

Due to a knee injury, he was discharged from his national service after 11 months. Thereafter he owned two sports shops in Stourbridge and later returned to help run the family newsagent's business. A keen golfer, he was a member at Dudley, Stourbridge and Enville Golf Clubs. In July 1959 he had married Judith Foley. They had celebrated nearly 60 years of marriage at the time of his death in 2019.

# KIMBER

## SIMON JULIAN SPENCER KIMBER – RIGHT-HAND BAT, RIGHT-ARM FAST-MEDIUM

Born: Ormskirk, Lancashire, 6 October 1963

*Portrait of Simon Kimber.*

First-class matches for Worcestershire: 2

- versus Oxford University, The Parks, Oxford, 22, 23, 24 May 1985
- versus Cambridge University, Fenner's, Cambridge, 12, 13, 14 June 1985

Innings: 1; Not out: 1; Runs: 14; Highest score: 14 not out; Caught: 1; Wickets: 3; Best bowling: 3-40

*Against Oxford University, Worcestershire won by an innings and 22 runs. Winning the toss and fielding, Worcestershire dismissed Oxford for 105 with Richard Illingworth taking 6-9 from 13 overs. Kimber's seven overs cost 18 runs.*

138

*Worcestershire replied with 310-9 declared, with half-centuries for Martin Weston (97) and David Banks (76), with Kimber finishing 14 not out.*

*The students were dismissed for 183 with only captain Andrew Miller putting up any resistance with 72. Illingworth was the pick of the bowlers once more, taking 7-50. Kimber again went wicketless, conceding 14 runs in his two overs.*

*Against Cambridge University, match drawn. While Worcestershire entertained Zimbabwe at New Road, seven players were given first-class debuts in the match at Cambridge.*

*Thanks to half-centuries from acting captain and wicket-keeper David Humphries (62 not out) and David Banks (50 not out) a crisis was averted and Worcestershire posted 216-5 declared. Due to bad weather the University replied with 143-6. However, it gave Kimber the opportunity to take 3-40, including the wickets of Tony Lea and Peter Roebuck.*

Simon Kimber was educated at Thomas More School in Durban. He then studied, for insurance examinations and achieved an national qualifications framework level 6 through the University of South Africa to be certified as an associate of the Insurance Institute of South Africa. As early as 1983 he worked in the family's 'short-term insurance' brokerage firm, Ron Kimber Insurance Brokers, where he still works as managing director.

He began his cricket career playing for Hampshire second XI against Sussex second XI in June 1983. He played four more matches in 1984 and in June that year, while playing for Dudley in the Birmingham League, also played for Worcestershire's Club and Ground XI. He made his first appearance for Worcestershire seconds in an exciting four-run defeat to Warwickshire and played five additional matches that season finishing with 18 wickets at 23 apiece. In the game against Leicestershire he took the wicket of Mike Haysman, the well-respected broadcaster.

*Worcestershire Club and Ground XI in 1984.*
*Kimber is on the front row, extreme left.*
*Standing at the back on the extreme left,*
*is Harshad Patel who features elsewhere in this publication.*

Kimber's first senior match for Worcestershire was in a friendly game against Scotland at New Road on 20 April 1985. Scotland won by five wickets but he claimed the wicket of their captain Richard Swan for 75.

He told me that he enjoyed being at New Road and that he spent a lot of time with coach Basil D'Oliveira. He recalled the start of the 1985 season when he was included in the squad of 12 to play against Middlesex at Lord's in the opening match of the Championship season: '*I travelled to Lord's with Kapil Dev in Duncan Fearnley's Rolls Royce and heard some very interesting stories about Kapil. I remember it was bitterly cold and snowed early on in the morning and then again later on as snow ended play early on day one.*' Kapil went on to score exactly 100; however, in a game in which both Neal Radford and Steve Rhodes made their first-class debuts for Worcestershire, they were beaten by eight wickets.

Following his two, first-class matches for Worcestershire, Kimber returned to the seconds where he played a further seven matches, leaving the Club at the end of 1985.

He started the 1986 season with a match for Derbyshire seconds against Nottinghamshire seconds and then spent the remainder of the season playing in the Manchester and District Cricket Association. In the winter of 1986–87 he played club cricket for Durban Collegians and first-class cricket for Natal B, taking a then career best of 4-76 in his debut game against Eastern Province B.

From 1987 to 1989, Kimber played 14 first-class and 28 second-team games for Sussex. His career best with the bat was 54 against Nottinghamshire at Eastbourne in August 1987, before he was caught and bowled by Richard Hadlee. His best return with the ball was 3-44 against Derbyshire at Horsham in June 1988.

His game for Natal against Transvaal in a Castle Currie Cup game in December 1990 was one of his fondest memories in cricket and the biggest highlight of his career: '*I was making my debut for Natal as was Jonty Rhodes; Kim Hughes the Australian was our captain. Transvaal declared on 270-6 and we were bowled out cheaply for 197. We bowled Transvaal out for 124 and I took 3-36 including the prize wicket of their captain, Clive Rice, who I had lbw for 10. We scored 199 for the loss of just four wickets to win. It was an outstanding achievement because the 'Transvaal Mean Machine' as it was known, had not lost at the Wanderers for many years.*'

Kimber continued to play for both Natal and Natal B until December 1993. His best return for Natal was 4-26 against Northern Transvaal at Centurion Park in February 1991, while his best figures for Natal B were 5-63 off 23 overs against Transvaal B. The game was played at the Wanderers Number 3 Oval, Johannesburg in January 1992 and ended in a draw.

*Simon Kimber in 2020.*

# KRIKKEN

## BRIAN EGBERT KRIKKEN – LEFT-HAND BAT, WICKET-KEEPER

Born: Horwich, Lancashire, 26 August 1946

*Portrait of Brian Krikken.*

First-class matches for Worcestershire: 1 versus Cambridge University, Seth Somers Park, Halesowen, 21, 23, 24 June 1969

Innings: 1; Not out: 0; Runs: 4; Highest score: 4; Caught: 2; Stumped: 0

*Worcestershire won by 10 wickets. Winning the toss and batting, Cambridge were bowled out for 80 with Doug Slade taking 5-31 from 16 overs. One of those wickets was Roger Knight, whom Krikken caught behind for nought.*

*Worcestershire replied with 147, an innings held together by Alan Ormrod with 56, the only batsman to score a half-century in the game. Krikken's contribution was four before he was bowled by Anand Bhatia.*

*Dismissing the students for 120 in their second innings, Norman Gifford had figures of 5-54 from 20 overs. Requiring 54 to win, Ron Headley 29 and Glenn Turner 24, helped Worcestershire to their target with a day to spare.*

Krikken's love of cricket was inherited from his father who had kept wicket for Horwich and Eagley Cricket Clubs. It was during his education at Rivington and Blackrod Grammar School that his skill as a cricketer was recognised. In 1962 he was selected for the Lancashire Federation under-19s, when he was barely 16, and in August 1965 was chosen for the English Schools against the Welsh Schools at Trent Bridge, a game which English Schools won by nine wickets.

After leaving school Krikken worked in a bank but didn't enjoy it: *'I preferred the "crack" on the shop floor; that was my type of environment. As a result, I went to work for a company called Automotive Products (part of the Lockheed Group) as an accounts clerk, a cashier and then a wages controller.'*

His first Minor Counties game was for Lancashire seconds against Cheshire in May 1965. In an innings and six-run victory, a strong Lancashire side included David Lloyd, Peter Lever, Sonny Ramadhin, Harry Pilling and Ken Snellgrove. The following month, Krikken made his debut in the Second XI Championship for Lancashire against Derbyshire, claiming two catches but being dismissed for a duck.

Krikken's team-mates nicknamed him 'Doctor', which alluded to the infamous murderer Dr Crippen. He played his league cricket for Westhoughton and had spells with Horwich, Eagley and Tonge Cricket Clubs, and in June 1966 represented the Bolton Cricket League in a game versus the Birmingham and District Cricket League, helping Bolton to a 15-run win. He showed his excellence with the gloves by making three stumpings and taking a catch, two of his victims being future Worcestershire team-mates Brian Brain and Bob Carter.

He was a combative wicket-keeper and in his book about the Bolton League author Arthur Hargreaves said of Krikken: *'the heavens ring with his almost continuous and loud appealing'*, something Krikken's son Karl inherited from his father during his first-class career with Derbyshire.

*Krikken, on the right,*
*opening for Westhoughton CC with Derek Hamblett.*

Krikken made his first-class debut for Lancashire against Oxford University at The Parks on 8 June 1966. He had the satisfaction of taking three catches, including Peter Gibbs (who later played for Derbyshire) for a duck off Peter Lever who claimed 5-43. He took two more catches off Lever in his second and final first-class game for Lancashire, which was against Scotland at Old Trafford in July 1967. With Farokh Engineer the incumbent wicket-keeper, Krikken decided he needed a fresh opportunity if his ambitions to be a regular professional cricketer were to be realised.

The opportunity presented itself in July 1968 when he made his debut for Worcestershire second XI in the drawn game against Derbyshire. On 29 November 1968 the *Birmingham Daily Post* reported that '*Worcestershire CCC have engaged Brian Krikken, the 23-year-old wicket-keeper/batsman, who left Lancashire at the end of last season at his own request. Joe Lister commented: "He will specially be registered if required, or if performances warrant consideration for the county side."*'

Krikken continued to play for Worcestershire seconds and was verbally offered a contract although it never materialised. He said: '*When I first came to New Road I stayed in the YMCA for three weeks. I didn't have a car and my wife was pregnant. Karl was then born and Brian Brain helped to find us a bungalow but Karl was seriously ill with mastoiditis when he was very little and we found it hard to settle. Added to that, I had a bust up with Joe Lister [the club secretary and second XI captain] on two occasions; we just didn't see eye to eye. As he was second-team captain it made life very tricky.'*

He recalled another story concerning Joe Lister: '*Blakeney won the Derby in 1969 and Joe had backed this horse for over 12 months at long odds ... and it won. We had been practising and were sitting in the dressing room when a very drunk Joe Lister walked in.*

'*The groundsman was rolling the wicket for the next day's game and Joe decided to take over from him. Keith Wilkinson, who was on the ground staff, was helping to repair the net area on the outfield at the far side of New Road near the scoreboard.*

'*Lister lost control of the roller and headed off towards Keith, who had his back to the action. Just in time, he got out of the way despite him not hearing us yell at him to move. Joe went straight through the fence and made a terrible mess, much to our amusement.*'

Krikken says he had very happy memories of his time at New Road, especially the friendships formed with fellow aspiring players Roy Barker and Keith Baylis. He returned to play in the Bolton League until his early 40s. He played for British Aerospace with Karl (until he moved to Astley Bridge) and played against the great Pakistanis Javed Miandad and Mudassar Nazar. The British Aerospace Cricket Ground is now the Bolton Wanderers Football Club Academy Ground.

Regarded as one of the finest wicket-keepers ever to play in the Bolton League, Krikken was recently named in the best all time League XI and is seventh – with 422 dismissals – in the list of wicket-keeping dismissals. He maintained his local connections, coaching Westhoughton and Horwich until he reached 60.

*Boxing Day charity game at Farnworth Social Circle CC, late-1960s*
*– Krikken is on his haunches on the right.*

Aged 45 he was made redundant and went to work for Booth Industries, a steel company making heavy duty steel doors for oil rigs and for use in the channel tunnel. He worked for them for 20 years running the stores, and retired at 65.

In retirement he is an expert grower of tomatoes and chrysanthemums, a skill he says he inherited from his grandfather, a keen horticulturalist of Dutch origin. Krikken's other passion is his lifelong support for Wigan Athletic Football Club.

# MOHAMMED

## AMJAD MOHAMMED – LEFT-HAND BAT, SLOW LEFT ARM

Born: Marston Green, Birmingham, 23 March 1971

*Amjad Mohammed during his debut game.*

First-class matches for Worcestershire:1 versus South Africa A, New Road, Worcester, 9, 10, 11, 12 August 1996

Innings: 2; Not out: 0; Runs: 8; Highest score: 7; Caught: 0; Wickets: 0; Best bowling: 0-25

*South Africa A won by 172 runs. Dismissing South Africa A for 202, Worcestershire were then bowled out for just 77, Gary Gilder, with figures of 8-22 being the main destroyer. Batting again, the visitors were bowled out for 325 with Meyrick Pringle, batting at number eight, scoring 105. Mohammed only bowled four overs in the visitors' second innings, which cost 25 runs.*

*Requiring 451 to win, Worcestershire were dismissed for 278, with half-centuries from David Leatherdale (73) and Steve Rhodes (51) preventing further embarrassment. James Ralph was also making his debut for Worcestershire in this game and features elsewhere in this publication.*

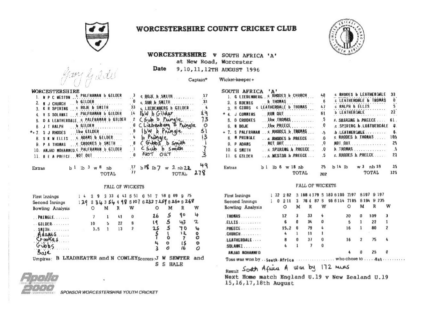

*Match scorecard signed by Gary Gilder.*

As a 17-year-old, having attended Small Heath School in Birmingham, Mohammed took 5-21 for Warwickshire Young Amateurs who dismissed Nottinghamshire Cricket Association under-19s for just 116 in a Hilda Overy Trophy game at Caythorpe. This was Mohammed's debut and he cites taking a hat-trick in this innings as one of the highlights of his career. He continued his cricketing education with Smethwick in the Birmingham League.

Between 1989 and 1996 Mohammed made regular second XI appearances for Warwickshire, Derbyshire, Somerset and Worcestershire. In all he played 18 second XI games for Worcestershire – 13 in the Championship, taking 24 wickets at 29.75 with a best of 7-71 against Northants at New Road – and five in The Bain Hogg Trophy, taking six wickets at 23.33.

In 1995 Mohammed, claimed 2-35 playing for Devon – captained by Peter Roebuck and with Chris Read as wicket-keeper – in the 82-run victory against Glamorgan seconds at Instow.

Following his sole appearance for Worcestershire in 1996, Mohammed played one game for Cornwall in 1998 against Cheshire in a Minor Counties game at Ladycross, Werrington, taking no wickets in either innings.

With a keen interest in coaching, Mohammed played for Torquay in Devon and worked in retail, continuing thereafter to play cricket for Berkswell in the Warwickshire Cricket League Premier Division.

He says his greatest achievement is to have memorised the holy book of Islam, The Qur'an, which consists of 6,666 verses. He now works in the Birmingham area where he runs his own business as a driving instructor.

*Mohammed taking the field during his debut game.*

# MOULE

### HARRY GEORGE MOULE – RIGHT-HAND BAT

Born: Brinton Park, Kidderminster, Worcestershire, 23 December 1921

Died: Barnstaple, North Devon, 15 June 2016

*Portrait of Harry Moule.*

First-class matches for Worcestershire: 1 versus Cambridge University, New Road, Worcester, 25, 26, 27 June 1952

Innings: 2; Not out: 0; Runs: 102; Highest score: 57; Caught: 0; Did not bowl

*Cambridge University won by six wickets. Worcestershire were dismissed for 295, with half-centuries for George Dews (54) and Roly Jenkins (85). Opening the batting, Harry's contribution was 45 before being run out. Dismissing the students for 185 (Mike Stevenson 53), Jenkins claimed 8-82.*

*Worcestershire declared their second innings on 262-6, thanks to 88 not out from Bob Broadbent and Moule, who was stumped by Gerry Alexander off Raman Subba Row, for a creditable 57. Cambridge were set a challenging 373 to win; however, Subba Row (68) and David Sheppard, with a magnificent 239 not out, ensured a six-wicket win for the visitors. Bill Goodreds was also making his debut for Worcestershire in the game and features elsewhere in this publication.*

Harry Moule's daughter Lynda said of her father that: '*he loved all his sport and played cricket as soon as he could stand up*'. Judging by his neat stance, this early picture of him appears to justify that statement.

After being educated at King Charles I Grammar School in Kidderminster, Moule trained as a draughtsman and by this stage was already a member of Kidderminster Cricket Club's second XI, who were Birmingham League Second Division champions in 1939.

*Moule as a youngster.*

During the War, he had intended to join the Royal Air Force but was rejected after failing a colour eye test, subsequently working as a draughtsman at Short Brothers in Rochester, Kent. He helped with the design of Short's Sunderland Flying Boat Patrol Bomber and it was at Short's that he met Emily, who was working as a telephonist; they were married in 1945.

Still playing for Kidderminster, on 6 July 1940 Moule helped re-write the League record books. In a letter I received from him in 2004 he recalled the moment in some detail: *'There were three brothers in the Humphries family, all of whom played for Worcestershire, Gerald, Cedric and Norman, who also played for Devon. Cedric was killed in World War Two [and was] a fine batsman who shared a record partnership with me of 313 for the first wicket at Portland Road against Mitchells and Butlers in 1940. Cedric made 156 not out and I made 113 not out.'*

At the end of the War Harry and Emily moved back to Kidderminster to live with his parents in the village of Chaddesley Corbett. He then worked as a draughtsman at Longbridge in Birmingham, for Austin Motors.

In 1950, Kidderminster, in their centenary year, were crowned Birmingham League Champions. The side contained four Worcestershire players; the great Somerset and England all-rounder Arthur Wellard was their professional and, despite being in his late-40s, took all 10 wickets for 33 runs in a League game against Stourbridge.

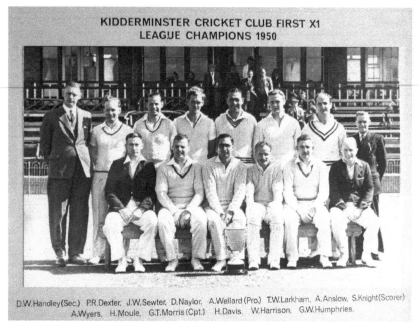

KIDDERMINSTER CRICKET CLUB FIRST X1
LEAGUE CHAMPIONS 1950

D.W.Handley(Sec.)  P.R.Dexter,  J.W.Sewter,  D.Naylor,  A.Wellard (Pro.)  T.W.Larkham,  A.Anslow,  S.Knight(Scorer)
A.Wyers,  H.Moule,  G.T.Morris (Cpt.)  H.Davis,  W.Harrison,  G.W.Humphries.

*Worcestershire CCC connections in this picture –
Jim Sewter, first-team scorer (1979 to 1997), plus Trevor Larkham,
Alick Wyers, Harry Moule and Gerald Humphries,
all of whom played first-class cricket for the County.*

The 1950 season proved to be an outstanding one for Moule. On 17 May he finished on 112 not out as Kidderminster made light work of Moseley's 202-6 declared. They closed on 203-3 to win by seven wickets.

On 8 July Smethwick were dismissed for 200; however, Moule and Alick Wyers knocked off the runs in an unbroken opening stand of 201. Moule finished on 103 and Wyers on 92. The following month, in response to Dudley's 218-6 declared, the same two batsmen helped Kidderminster to a nine-wicket victory. In an opening partnership of 216 – just three runs short of their victory target – Moule was dismissed for 119 while Wyers closed on 92 not out.

Moule's daughter commented about his undoubted ability: '*My mum always said Dad could have played professionally and was certainly good enough. However, my eldest sister was born in 1948 and the other sister in 1952 so it was not viable.*'

*Moule – on the left – with Alick Wyers having put on 216 for the first wicket against Dudley.*

On 22 May 1954, Moule nearly carried his bat in an extraordinary game against Moseley. After a rain-delayed start Moseley staggered to 136-7 declared, leaving Kidderminster just two hours of batting. Bert Latham took 10-37 as Kidderminster were dismissed for 80. Moule had held out until the score reached 73, when a beauty of a ball bowled him for 32.

He went on to captain Kidderminster for a while before moving to Old Hill, where he helped them win the Championship in 1960, scoring 624 runs in his 21st season in the League.

Moule was an excellent squash player and played to a high standard well into his 40s. He was also an avid follower of Aston Villa but also continued to closely follow the fortunes of Worcestershire CCC.

In his 70s Moule moved to Fremington in North Devon to be near to Lynda, and watched cricket at Instow in the company of the former Gloucestershire player and world-famous umpire David Shepherd.

In October 2010 he made the headlines again when the *North Devon Gazette* reported that: 'Over 65s get to grips with the net.'

Moule had found out about the event, Get Online Week, after spotting a newspaper article and attending his local Pathfinder Learning Centre. Supported by the Post Office, UK Online Centres and the BBC, it was designed to help the over-65s get to grips with computers and the internet.

The newspaper reported that: *'88-year-old Harry Moule was one of a number of self-confessed "internet virgins" taking advantage of the supported computer access sessions at Barnstaple Post Office.*

*'Mr Moule, a former county cricketer who played for Worcestershire in the 1950s, even used the session to discover a Wikipedia page devoted to his cricketing past.*

*'He said: "At first it was very difficult but I got used to it, and now I can follow the cricket online and email my family in New Zealand.*

*'"It's great – I even watched a video of my granddaughter's wedding on YouTube."'*

*Moule at Barnstaple Post Office.*

At 91, Harry gave up another his other favourite sports, swimming, and, as his eyesight deteriorated, also gave up driving. Four years later his story came to an end, which is described with some poignant words from his daughter: '*We knew he wasn't long for this world when he didn't talk about the cricket or the Villa! He swapped the remote control for an old cricket ball I found in a wardrobe and held it in his hand during the last few days of his life. Dad's funeral was cricket-themed and he went off the pitch wearing his Worcester tie.*'

# MUNN

## REGINALD GEORGE MUNN – RIGHT-HAND BATSMAN

Born: Madresfield, Worcestershire, 20 August 1869
Died: Virginia Water, Surrey, 12 April 1947

*Portrait of George Munn.*

First-class matches for Worcestershire: 1 versus MCC, Lord's Cricket Ground, 26, 27, 28 July 1900

Innings: 1; Not out: 0; Runs: 2; Highest score: 2; Caught: 0; Did not bowl

*Match drawn. MCC won the toss and elected to bat, scoring 313 all out, with Billy Gunn from Nottinghamshire top-scoring with 110.*

*In reply, Worcestershire were bowled out for 336 thanks to Fred Bowley's 98, and 81 from Fred Wheldon. Batting at number eight, George Munn scored two before he became one of Dick Pougher's eight victims at the cost of 151 runs.*

*MCC closed on 91-3 in their second innings, with the rare event of R.E. Foster opening the bowling with 'Dick' Pearson. Foster took 2-34 from 14 overs.*

George Munn's father, the Reverend George Shaw Munn, was the rector of St Mary, Madresfield in Worcestershire for 49 years, from 1856 to 1905.

Educated at Haileybury College, George Munn spoke fluent French and German. He first represented a side from Worcestershire when he played for Worcestershire under-17s against Herefordshire under-17s at Hampton Court, Leominster in August 1885. They were defeated by an innings and 82 runs, with Munn dismissed for two in each innings.

Having 'passed out' from the Royal Military Academy at Sandhurst, in 1889, Munn was commissioned as second lieutenant serving with the 1st Battalion of the Sherwood Foresters. He was promoted to lieutenant on 1 November 1890. A career soldier, he was to serve with great distinction. In September 1891 he was admitted to the Indian Staff Corps and attached to the 36th Sikhs of the Bengal Infantry.

Between 1890 and 1893 he made regular appearances for the Worcestershire Club and Ground team and in August 1893 top-scored with 53 in the game versus Stourbridge at Amblecote.

The same year, R.G. Munn's XI met Boughton Park at Malvern College. Munn's XI scored 151 (Munn run out 15) and dismissed Boughton Park for 104, with, a 19-year-old 'Plum' Warner carrying his bat for 40 not out, as Munn's XI won by 47 runs.

Munn played regularly at Boughton Park during the annual cricket week festivals held there. This picture from 1893 shows 11 of the players who took part during the week.

*Back row, left to right: G.E. Bromley-Martin, R.W. Rice,
E.E. Lea, A.W. Isaac, E.L. Wheeler.
Middle row, left to right: H.C. Isaac, R.G. Munn,
E.G.M. Carmichael, W.S. Ryan, Miss A.V. Isaac (scorer)
Front row, left to right: P.H. Latham, P.F. Warner.*

Munn served with the Chitral Relief Force in 1895, returning home to play cricket in 1896, and in May he was in the victorious Gentlemen of Worcestershire side which beat Emeriti by 70 runs at Boughton Park. In June he represented Worcestershire who played Northumberland in the Minor Counties Championship game at Kidderminster, which the home side won by 119 runs.

Later in the season, playing in the Birmingham League for Kidderminster against Dudley (at Kidderminster), he top-scored with 31 before being run out as the home side won by one wicket.

In 1897–98 Munn returned to the North West Frontier of India with the 36th Sikhs as adjutant to Lieutenant-Colonel Haughton, and it was there that he was involved in some of the fiercest fighting. On one occasion, with an overwhelming enemy force approaching the village of Gulistan, Haughton and his men were out-numbered as they tried to support their men in the many smaller outposts over the Samana Range.

*Officers of the 36th Sikhs, Tirah, 1897, Munn is seated on the left.*

Taken from the *Indian Frontier War 1897* by Lionel James, the account of the action makes for interesting reading: '*There was some close fighting in the dark and the village was cleared, the men showing great determination to hold it overnight. After a short while, three Afridis, evidently lying in wait, suddenly sprang from the middle of them and darted off. Munn pushed his sword through one and left it there. However, a short time later, some of the enemy crept up close and fired a volley, wounding Munn in the hand.*' Recovering from his injury, Munn was posted to the 2nd Battalion on 5 December 1899.

On 17 and 18 August 1900, while home on leave, Munn played for MCC against Devon at Gras Lawn, Exeter, top-scoring with 55 as the match was drawn.

Having previously been promoted to captain, from November 1901 he served as aide-de-camp to Colonel Charles Egerton, Commander of the Punjab Frontier Force. He was mentioned in a dispatch from Egerton dated 4 July 1902, following operations against the Mahsud Waziris. He was also admitted to the Stewart Lodge of the Freemasons in Rawalpindi.

On 6 June 1906, Munn married Helen Muriel Jeddere-Fisher at St John's Church, Dormansland, Surrey and the following year was appointed a major with the 36th Sikhs.

Munn's last game of cricket was in 1908 for MCC in the drawn game against East Grinstead in August. He played alongside Arthur Conan Doyle, the famed creator of Sherlock Holmes. Conan Doyle took a single first-class wicket in his career, none other than that of the great W.G. Grace.

Munn continued to serve with the Indian Army during the World War One. On 3 July 1915 he was admitted to Millbank Hospital suffering with a gunshot wound to the leg, but was discharged two days later. He was subsequently promoted to lieutenant-colonel.

In January 1919 *The London Gazette* announced that: '*The King has been graciously pleased to give directions for the following promotions in and appointments to the Most Distinguished Order of Saint Michael and Saint George (CMG) for services rendered in connection with the War. Dated 1st January 1919 – Lt. Col. Reginald George Munn.*'

After the War, Munn began to take an active role in politics. In the 1920s, Charles Everard, a local activist for the Conservative Party – and an Urban District Councillor – had become disillusioned with that Party and on 15 May 1925 joined with Munn to form the East Grinstead branch of the British Fascists.

In 1936 Munn helped found the Forty Club and was appointed an honorary fellow. It was the idea of Henry Grierson and the initial intention was to enable good cricket players to enjoy cricket in their middle age. That remit changed and the Club decided to play (and still does) matches against schools with the aim of developing and encouraging cricket in schools.

# PALMER

## CECIL HOWARD PALMER – RIGHT-HAND BATSMAN

Born: East Worldham, Hampshire, 14 July 1873
Died: (in action) near Hill Q, Gallipoli, Turkey, 26 July 1915

*Portrait of Cecil Palmer.*

First-class matches for Worcestershire: 1 versus Oxford University, New Road, Worcester, 7, 8, 9 July 1904

Innings: 2; Not out: 1; Runs: 116; Highest score: 75 not out; Caught: 0; Did not bowl

*Oxford University won by three wickets. Winning the toss and batting first, Worcestershire were dismissed for 490. William Burns with 165, scored in three hours, was the mainstay of the innings and was well supported by H.K. Foster (53) and Reginald Brinton (72 not out). Palmer was lbw to William Evans for 41. Evans was an all-rounder who had played six matches for Worcestershire in 1901.*

*Oxford replied with 345, thanks to 107 not out from Kenneth Carlisle and 75 from John Raphael. George Wilson with 5-107 was the pick of the Worcestershire bowlers.*

*Worcestershire declared their second innings on 254-6, with John Cuffe making 51 and Palmer, a debut half-century of 75 not out.*

*Requiring 400 to win, the students pulled off a fine victory. It was made possible with centuries from Raphael (111) and George Bennett (131). They were well supported by Carlisle who scored his second half-century of the game (71).*

Cecil Palmer's father was the vicar of East Worldham in Hampshire when Cecil was born, in 1873. Educated at Ashampstead, he later studied at Radley College between 1888 and 1891. As a schoolboy he became a prefect and played for the Radley cricket XIs of 1890 and 1891 and was also in the football XI.

*Palmer playing for Radley College first XI, 1891.*

After leaving Radley in 1891 Palmer served in the militia in the 3rd Battalion of the York and Lancaster Regiment. He took up his commission in the Worcestershire Regiment in 1894 and on

1 February 1901 was promoted to lieutenant. He served in the Mounted Infantry Detachment of the Worcesters in the 2nd South African Boer War from 1899–1900 (and was promoted to captain on 20 June) and, following action in Orange Free State, was mentioned in despatches four times, receiving the Queen's Medal with four clasps.

In July 1899 Palmer made his first-class debut for Hampshire in the game against Sussex at Hove, and in his second game against Yorkshire at Bradford scored a second-innings 64 in a drawn game. He was described as a sound bat and a brilliant cover fielder. He played two further games for Hampshire in 1901.

His skill as a cricketer was undoubted and in 1903 he made 102 and 127 for the Gentlemen of Worcestershire versus the Gentlemen of Warwickshire at Edgbaston, and when home on leave also played for Kidderminster in the Birmingham League.

On 28 November 1903, he married Hilda Beatrice Hall at Alton Parish Church. They had two boys – John, born in Barbados, and Gerald, born in Kidderminster, as was his daughter Philippa.

The following year, he made the switch from Hampshire to Worcestershire and played his only first-class game for the County in July. Later in the season he had the unique distinction of also playing against Worcestershire while representing Hampshire once more. In a high-scoring game he was dismissed twice by Ted Arnold for scores of three and nought.

Playing for the 1st Battalion of the Worcester Regiment against Warwickshire Club and Ground in September 1908 he scored six and 43 in the drawn game. He continued to enjoy his sport and won the singles in the Divisional Lawn Tennis Tournament at Aldershot, and when in Burma beat the American tennis champion. With his doubles partner Guy Davidge (who appears elsewhere in this publication), he won several local tournaments.

By 1912 he had risen to the rank of major and at the beginning of 1914 was in charge of the depot at Worcester and beginning to look towards retirement. However, instead, in 1914, he was given the temporary rank of lieutenant-colonel and placed in command of the newly created 9th Battalion of the Royal Warwickshire Regiment.

*Regiment photo – Palmer is fourth from the right,
on the front row next to the regimental mascot.*

The entry of Turkey into the War led to the decision to send three divisions to the Dardanelles. In the battle of 28 April 1915 the Allied Armies of Britain, Australia and New Zealand won a foothold at the south end of the peninsula of Gallipoli around Cape Helles. If more ground was to be taken it was clear that many reinforcements would be required.

Among the three divisions sent out from England was the 9th Service Battalion of the Royal Warwickshire Regiment, commanded by Lieutenant-Colonel Palmer, and the 9th Worcesters.

*Lieutenant-Colonel Palmer – 9th Royal Warwickshire Regiment.*

On 7 June 1915 they received orders to sail to the Mediterranean, and travelling by train via Frimley Station to Avonmouth Docks in Bristol boarded HMT *Royal Edward* on 17 June. The ship steamed via Malta and Alexandria arriving at Mudros on the Greek island of Lemnos on 9 July. All of the units assembled in preparation for landing at Gallipoli, and on 13 July the 9th Battalion Royal Warwickshire Regiment landed on Beach V near Cape Helles.

On 25 July near Hill Q, Commanding Officer Lieutenant-Colonel Palmer was killed by a sniper. He was buried in Trolley Ravine and a wooden cross was placed at his grave by the men of his regiment.

In a letter to Lieutenant-Colonel Palmer's widow, Major-General Shaw, commanding the 13th Division wrote; '*It may help a little to soften the blow to know how highly we thought of him and what good work he was doing for his country. He had made his battalion and made it a good one, and that is a record of which you may all be proud.*'

A poignant obituary appeared in the *Kidderminster Times and Advertiser*. This extract from it was written by Major Gordon, second in command: '*We all deplore the death of our gallant Colonel most grievously. We all loved and respected him. I don't know how we shall get on without him; he was the very soul of the regiment.*'

In 2015 Lieutenant-Colonel Palmer's granddaughter, four grandsons and their wives travelled to Turkey to commemorate his death. They spent three days touring the battlefield, which is now a national park. In a moving visit, they paid their respects at the Helles Memorial and then they stopped at the precise place where he fell to lay a single poppy in his memory.

# PATEL

## HARSHAD VALLABHBHAI PATEL – RIGHT-HAND BAT, RIGHT-ARM OFF-BREAK

Born: Nairobi, Kenya, 29 January 1964

*Portrait of Harshad Patel.*

First-class matches for Worcestershire: 1 versus Cambridge University, Fenner's, 12, 13, 14 June 1985

Innings: 1; Not out: 0; Runs: 39; Highest score: 39; Caught: 0; Did not bowl

*Match drawn. While Worcestershire entertained Zimbabwe at New Road, seven players were given first-class debuts in the match at Cambridge. Three of them, Lawrence Smith, Stuart Lampitt and Paul Bent, all subsequently played Championship*

*cricket. Four of them – Harshad Patel along with Mel Hussain, Mike Scothern and Brian Barrett, who feature elsewhere in this publication, were not afforded the same opportunity.*

*Thanks to half-centuries from acting captain and wicket-keeper, David Humphries (62 not out) and David Banks (50 not out) – plus a polished 39 from Harshad Patel – a crisis was averted and Worcestershire posted 216-5 declared. Due to bad weather the University replied with 143-6.*

Harshad Patel's connections to Worcestershire are strong. His cousin Dipak Patel, the stylish, elegant all-rounder, played 234 first-class matches for the County between 1976 and 1986 before emigrating to New Zealand.

Educated at George Salter High School in West Bromwich and Rowley Regis College in Dudley, Patel began his Birmingham League career with West Bromwich Dartmouth. On 14 July 1981 he made his first appearance in Worcestershire colours playing for Worcestershire under-25s against Gloucestershire under-25s in the Warwick Pool competition. During this time, he also played for Worcestershire's Club and Ground XI.

In 1983 he was a member of the Worcestershire side that lost the final of the under-25s' competition to Leicestershire in a game played at Edgbaston. With the scores level on 198, Leicestershire were deemed winners as they had lost five wickets compared to Worcestershire's eight. Patel scored 44 while Australian Greg Matthews, playing in the UK as part of the Esso Scholarship, scored 54.

In the mid-1980s Patel shared a house with Graeme Hick and one of his main responsibilities, he told me, was to act as Basil D'Oliveira's chauffeur. Following his debut game in 1985 he continued to play for the second XI but was released at the end of that season and played second XI cricket for Derbyshire in 1986.

*Warwick Pool side.*
*Back row, left to right:*
*David Slater, Steve McEwan, Andy Webster, Phil Newport,*
*David Banks, Peter Moores, Ricardo Ellcock.*
*Front row, left to right:*
*Steve Watkins (who appears elsewhere in this publication),*
*Mark Scott, Harshad Patel, Greg Matthews, Martin Weston.*

In spite of that, he had fond memories of his debut game and recalled an incident involving teammate Brian Barrett: '*After an evening out in Cambridge, Brian took a bike to get back to the hotel. During the next home game two policemen turned up in the New Road dressing room and asked Brian to step outside for questioning. He went very red in the face, only to find out that Paul Pridgeon had asked two policemen friends to call in as a wind-up!*'

During the winter, Patel coached at Ellerslie Cricket Club in New Zealand and for the following two winters worked with David Banks as a regional coach, at Albany in Western Australia. Lifelong friends, Patel is godfather to David's son, Josh. Patel was now working for Jeavons Engineering in Tipton as a buyer. While there, he studied for a degree at Birmingham University and gained a 2:2 in business and finance.

Now playing Birmingham League cricket for Stourbridge, 1986 provided one of his proudest moments in cricket. In the final of the William Younger Cup they met Weston-super-Mare in the Final at Lord's. In reply to Weston's 175 all out (Stuart Lampitt – who played for Worcestershire from 1985 to 2002 – claiming 5-43) Stourbridge's scored 176-6 with Patel hitting 54 to help them to a four-wicket victory. He was to spend 10 years at Stourbridge.

Patel represented Staffordshire in the Minor Counties Championship from 1988 until 1990. His finest performance was in the match against Bedfordshire at Highfield in Leek in June 1988. Opening the batting with Steve Dean he scored 116 and 51 not out in a drawn game as Staffordshire failed to take the last two wickets to earn the victory. In August his run of form continued when he scored 120 not out in the drawn game against Suffolk, also at Leek.

Working next in Birmingham as a unit trust, equities and foreign exchange dealer with TD Waterhouse, a Canadian bank, he made the switch to Herefordshire for the 1992 season. In May that year he represented the England Amateur XI in a game against a strong Pakistan side which included Javed Miandad and Inzamam-ul-Haq.

After missing the 1993 season with a chronic back problem he regained his form and in 1995 scored 1,093 runs to become the first batsman for 16 seasons to break the 1,000 mark in the Minor Counties Championship.

His best run of form came between 5 and 10 July when he struck three centuries in four innings. Against Dorset in Weymouth he scored 135 not out and 105, then against Wiltshire at Marlborough hit 129.

The late-1990s saw a move to Old Hill in the Birmingham League. He rates his debut game against Smethwick on 10 July 1999 as his League highlight. Facing Worcestershire's Kabir Ali and the great Pakistani 'quick' Wasim Akram, he scored 57 as Old Hill scored 233 off their 60 overs. Wasim stole the show, however, striking 135 not out in just over an hour as Smethwick won by seven wickets.

In 2000, Herefordshire beat Cheshire by 42 runs to lift the Minor Counties Cricket Association Knockout Cup at Lord's, but perhaps Patel's most notable achievement came in 2001 when his man-of-the-match innings of 68 – part of a 129-run opening stand with Nathan Round – gained Herefordshire a three-wicket win over Middlesex in the Cheltenham and Gloucester Trophy game at the Luctonians Cricket Club ground. A strong Middlesex side included: Andrew Strauss, Owais Shah, Angus Fraser and Phil Tufnell.

*Patel lifting the Knockout Cup in 2000.*

While working as the England and Wales Cricket Board development manager for Herefordshire he had the opportunity to move to New Road to take up the role of cricket development officer with the Worcestershire Cricket Board; however, he left after a few months in post. He then moved to work as community development manager for Sandwell Council.

In 2002, Herefordshire shared the Minor Counties Championship with Norfolk, with Patel scoring 84 and 26 in the final. Continuing to play for West Bromwich Dartmouth, he cracked 152 not out in the final of the 2006 Cockspur Cup against Bromsgrove as they won by 90 runs.

Having played his last Minor Counties game in 2012 he was subsequently appointed coach of Herefordshire, who won the 2016 Minor Counties Knockout Cup. He became, and remains, the only player to have played in and coached a winning side. His tenure ended in 2017 as Herefordshire sought to include more local players in the team, which, according to Patel, would only work if the players were good enough. This prompted his departure after 26 years with the County.

*The coach with Herefordshire,*
*the 2016 Minor Counties Knockout Cup winners.*

Patel continued to play Birmingham League cricket for Himley, Smethwick, West Bromwich Dartmouth as captain, Old Hill and Stourbridge and still enjoys his cricket, having now played in the League for 46 seasons.

In September 2020 his outstanding contribution to cricket was recognised when he was inducted into the Wisden Club Cricketers Hall of Fame at number 41. He is now a test analyst for Fidelity National Information Service.

# PAWSON

### ALBERT GUY PAWSON – RIGHT-HAND BAT, WICKET-KEEPER

Born: Bramley, Leeds, 30 May 1888
Died: Lamerton, Devon, 25 February 1986

A. G. Pawson, Captain of Oxford in this Week's
Varsity Cricket Match

*Guy Pawson at the crease in 1910.*

First-class matches for Worcestershire: 1 versus Oxford University,
The Parks, Oxford, 11, 12, 13 June 1908

Innings: 2; Not out: 1; Runs: 12; Highest score: 12; Caught: 1;
Stumped: 3; Did not bowl

*Worcestershire won by 332 runs. In the first innings they were
indebted to George Simpson-Hayward who, out of a total of 185,
scored 105 in just 80 minutes.*

*Simpson-Hayward continued his excellent form and took 6-13 in the University's first innings of 85, with three of the batsmen being stumped by Guy Pawson. Batting for a second time, Worcestershire scored 362, William Burns striking 146 (in just over two hours at the crease). Leaving Oxford 463 to win, all-rounder Ted Arnold made light work of their second innings claiming 7-51 as Oxford were dismissed for 130, with Pawson contributing a catch to dismiss Trevor Bowring.*

*Eric Brownell, John Winnington and Freddy Grisewood were also making their debuts for Worcestershire in this game and feature elsewhere in this publication.*

The Pawson family were large-scale, woollen cloth manufacturers and merchants operating from the Stonebridge Mill at Farnley, near Otley in Yorkshire. Guy Pawson's grandfather, William Pawson, a wealthy landowner and magistrate, set up the business, and his father, Albert Henry Pawson, developed it further. He also bought Farnley Hall which became the family home.

Theirs was a family of influence and William Pawson was also one of the major landowners in South Norwood, Croydon, where he owned the Whitehorse Farm and the Beulah Spa grounds. Despite never being a resident his name survives through Pawson's Road, Pawson's Place and the Pawson's Arms pub, all of which can be found locally.

*The Pawson's Arms.*

Guy Pawson was educated at Woodcote House in Oxfordshire and at Winchester College where he played cricket for the first XI from 1905 until 1907. He was captain in his last two seasons. In the drawn game against Eton College in July 1906 he showed his promise as a wicket-keeper, claiming three stumpings in Eton's second innings. The following year he captained them to a nine-wicket victory, scoring 48 and 36.

*Pawson, captain of Winchester in 1906.*

Batting at number eight, in August 1907, he top-scored with 47 not out playing for the Public Schools (in a 12-a-side game) against MCC at Lord's, in a match they lost by an innings and 24 runs.

He 'went up' to Christ Church, Oxford and was awarded a bachelor of arts (2nd class honours) in history and took the special course in anthropology arranged for Sudan probationers. He was subsequently awarded the certificate in cultural anthropology in the Hilary term of 1911.

He made his first-class debut for the University against the Gentlemen of England in May 1908 and the following month made his first-class debut for Worcestershire, ironically, against the students. In 1982, I received a marvellous letter from Pawson, who was aged 94. Written in his own hand it was barely legible but once it had been deciphered revealed a remarkably vivid memory of the game some 74 years earlier. He wrote:

'Worcestershire arrived for the game without a wicket-keeper and I was asked to play for them. One of their bowlers was Simpson-Hayward, the last well-known lob bowler to play first-class cricket. He took six wickets for 13 runs, made a century and did not bowl in the second innings, presumably to save Oxford's face.

'I stumped three of the middle-order batsmen, one after the other, for six, nought and nought off his bowling. They had never played against a top-class lob bowler, someone who bowled at a reasonable pace and although his off-spin and top-spin balls came very quickly off the pitch – the leg break came more slowly but was unusually well disguised. Though I could pick it the moment he bowled it.'

The report in the *Worcester Journal* was favourable stating that: '*Pawson kept well and, strange as he was to Simpson-Hayward's bowling, his work of stumping three men was distinctly good.*' Pawson went on the receive his Blue in July and did so in each of the next three years, and he was the victorious captain in both 1910 and 1911; the 1910 game was remembered for the performance of Cambridge's Philip le Couteur, who scored 160 and had match figures of 11-66 as Oxford won by an innings and 126 runs. Towards the end of the season, Pawson played for Oxford University Authentics in their 53-run defeat to Northumberland's Club and Ground XI, in Jesmond.

Pawson was also a double-Blue for football, the *Oxford Times* stating that he was regarded as a '*speedy, dashing centre-forward whose play was characterised by energy and real hard work.*' He left Oxford in 1911 to join the Sudan Civil Service, which was regarded as one of Britain's three principal overseas services.

He married Helen Humphrey Lawson at Watlington in Oxfordshire on 3 June 1917; they were married for 62 years and had two sons – Philip, born in 1918, and Tony, born in 1921.

## Society at Lord's
### (WITH THE 'VARSITY CRICKET MATCH THROWN IN)

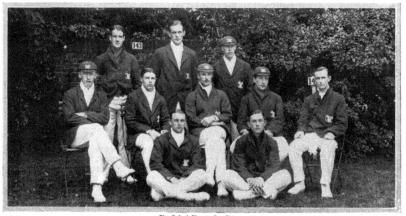

The Oxford Eleven—One Short

*Back Row:* J. L. S. Vidler, R. L. L. Braddell, H. S. Altham. *Sitting:* R. O. Lagden, R. H. Twining, A. J. Evans, A. G. Pawson, P. R. Le Couteur. *Front:* H. Brougham, I. P. F. Campbell

*Oxford University side for 1911. Pawson is seated, second from the right.*

*Guy and Helen Pawson.*

Tony Pawson was a fine sportsman in his own right. He played 69 first-class matches for Oxford University and Kent and played association football for Charlton Athletic, scoring on his League debut against Tottenham Hotspur. He also won the FA

Amateur Cup and was in the Great Britain football squad at the 1952 summer Olympic Games. He was a world-renowned fly fisherman, winning the world individual championship in 1984.

Guy Pawson was governor of the White Nile Province from 1931 until 1934 and secretary of the International Rubber Regulation committee between 1934 and 1942. He worked in the Colonial Office from 1942 until 1944, was then secretary of the International Rubber Study Group from 1944 to 1948, and served as its secretary-general from 1948 until 1960. He was awarded the 5th class of the Order of the Nile in 1924 and was appointed CMG (Most Distinguished Order of Saint George and Saint Michael) in the 1935 New Year Honours.

# RALPH

## JAMES TREVOR RALPH – RIGHT-HAND BAT, LEG-BREAK BOWLER

Born: Kidderminster, Worcestershire, 9 October 1975

*James Ralph on debut.*

First-class matches: 1 versus South Africa A, New Road, Worcester, 9, 10, 11, 12 August 1996

Innings: 2; Not out: 0; Runs: 0; Highest score: 0; Caught: 1; Did not bowl

*South Africa A won by 172 runs. After dismissing South Africa A for 202 (John Commins 61) Worcestershire were bowled out for just 77, with Ralph making a 13-ball duck. Gary Gilder, with figures of 8-22, was the main destroyer. Batting again, the visitors were bowled out for 325 with Meyrick Pringle, batting at number eight, scoring 105.*

*Requiring 451 to win, Worcestershire were dismissed for 278, with half-centuries from David Leatherdale (73) and Steve Rhodes (51) preventing further embarrassment. Ralph 'bagged a pair' as he was dismissed without score for a second time. His one consolation was a catch to dismiss Herschelle Gibbs in South Africa A's second innings. Amjad Mohammed was also making his debut for Worcestershire in this game and features elsewhere in this publication.*

Cricket was a way of life for Ralph as a youngster, his father Alan playing for the West Mercia Police Force team and his brother Stephen for Kidderminster. James Ralph recalls his first representative game for Worcestershire under-11s against Avon under-11s at Millfield School. He said: *'We got something like 120 and I was quite pleased as I got 41 not out, but Marcus Trescothick made 176 not out for Avon in the same game. When you're aged 10 or 11 you can struggle to get the ball off the square most of the time, but he was hitting sixes.'*

Educated at Harry Cheshire High School in Kidderminster, ironically, Ralph never played school cricket, choosing the local club route instead. He left school after completing his GCSEs and spent time in Australia, a visit he was to make on four other occasions, playing for Albany in Western Australia. He played in two country week finals and in one country cup final at the WACA in Perth.

He cites some of the finest local coaches who had the greatest influence on his early career: Rob Wood, Nick Haynes, John Huband, Dave Collins, Mark Scott (Worcestershire CCC 1981–1983) and especially, Keith Wilkinson (Worcestershire CCC 1969-1975). He regarded Keith as a fantastic captain to learn from as well as being a great coach.

Of Mark Scott, he said: *'His advice was invaluable in helping me get on the staff at Worcestershire and having him around at the time encouraged me to motivate myself properly. I remember playing a handful of games for Worcestershire under-19 Schools and getting three hundreds and an 80 against a strong Lancashire under-19 side.'*

Ralph played two matches for Worcestershire second XI in 1994 but it wasn't until two years later that he showed more promise and consistency in his batting. He ended the season with 604 runs, which included a century in the drawn game with Northamptonshire and half-centuries against Kent and Nottinghamshire and a well-made 83 not out against Yorkshire. The innings against Yorkshire had significance because their attack was led by Matthew Hoggard. It was this innings which resulted in Ralph being selected to make his first-class debut in August.

*Worcestershire CCC, 1996. James Ralph is on the back row, extreme right, and Amjad Mohammed (who appears elsewhere in this publication) is standing on the back row, extreme left.*

'Bagging a pair' in the game, Ralph assessed his performance with great honesty and told me: *'I don't think I did myself justice and to be honest I don't think I was ready then for the professional game. I hadn't really grown into myself then; a few years later I was much stronger and confident. In addition, I had played very little three-day cricket. I had been scoring runs regularly, I just didn't get the big scores that stand out. The immaturity in my game probably showed through in the one chance I was given.*

'From the sidelines it would not have looked good and I can remember, when I was told they weren't giving me a new contract, that this game was specifically mentioned. I felt disappointed with the Club as I believe that I deserved another year to show what I could have done.'

Returning to play League and Minor Counties cricket, Ralph also worked for Brinton's Carpets in their manufacturing and design department for four years and for the last 11 years has been a drayman for Hobsons Brewery, based in Cleobury Mortimer.

In 1998 Ralph began a long and fruitful career in Minor Counties cricket and in 1999, despite a one-run defeat, won the man-of-the-match award for his 89 in the Nat West Bank Trophy game against Hampshire Cricket Board at Wellington.

The following year – and Ralph regards this as the highlight of his career – he was named man of the match once more for a sparkling 102 not out in the Nat West Bank Trophy game against a full-strength Somerset side at Telford; however, the visitors won by 27 runs.

Modest in his assessment of his innings, he said: *'I was fairly lucky that I didn't face too many balls from Andy Caddick that day. I probably faced five balls off him, running them down to third man. I think if he hadn't been in the Somerset side we probably would have beaten them as his 10 overs cost only 27runs.'*

Regarded as a stylish middle-order batsman who could make batting look ridiculously easy, Ralph's best season in the Minor Counties Championship was in 2004 when in just six matches he scored 440 runs at an average of 73.33. In June he scored 102 against Oxfordshire and in July 138 against Dorset as Shropshire won both games.

He was captain between 2007 and 2009, joining Herefordshire for the following summer but then returning to Shropshire to be re-appointed captain for 2014 and 2015. The following season he became only the 13th player to have played 100 Minor Counties games for Shropshire, finally retiring at the end of 2017.

*Shropshire CCC versus Berkshire CCC in the Minor Counties Cricket Championship at Wormsley, 28 August, 2013.*
*Ralph is seated on the extreme right.*

He played a total of 103 games, scored 4,891 runs at an average of 31.97, with a highest score of 140 against Cornwall at St Austell in 2011. He took 42 wickets at 20.55 apiece and held on to 93 catches.

A consistent performer for Shropshire in one-day cricket, too, he clocked up a further 65 matches, scoring 1,099 runs at an average of 22.90. For the 2020 season, Ralph, along with former top-order batsman Tony Parton, joined Shropshire's new selection committee, which included the Club's newly appointed director of cricket, John Abrahams and player/coach Simon Kerrigan.

In 2009, Ralph returned to play for Kidderminster for one season. Subsequently he has played for several Shropshire clubs, including Ludlow, St George's, Bridgnorth (where he helped them win the Birmingham League Division Three and a double promotion to Division One), Shifnal, Broseley and now Quatt in the Shropshire County Cricket League.

In summing up his career, a forthright Ralph told me: '*I enjoyed my time at Worcester and had the pleasure, early in my career, to play against the likes of Anderson, Flintoff, Harmison and Collingwood. I was, though, probably in awe of where I was as I found myself in the changing room with all my heroes, like Hick, Moody, Curtis, D'Oliveira, Newport Haynes, Lampitt and Rhodes.*

*Ralph in action for Shropshire CCC.*

'I am honoured to be one of 13 cricketers to have represented Shropshire CCC in over 100 Championship games, having played for them for nearly 20 years. Shropshire have provided a pathway for many old team-mates into the first-class counties. You need a bit of luck in respect of which era you are playing in as comrades such as Harshad Patel, David Banks, Jonathan Wright, Ravi Nagra and Chris Burroughs could have played many more first-class games.'

# RILEY

## JACK RILEY – RIGHT-HAND BAT, SLOW LEFT ARM

Born: Accrington, Lancashire, 27 April 1927
Died: Preston, Lancashire, 28 May 2008

*Portrait of Jack Riley.*

First-class matches: 1 versus Cambridge University, Fenner's, 16, 18, 19 May 1953

Innings: 1; Not out: 0; Runs: 1; Highest score: 1; Caught: 1; Wickets: 3; Best bowling: 3-25

*Worcestershire won by seven wickets. Batting first, Cambridge were dismissed for 99 with Jack Riley taking 3-25 from 12.4 overs. His first wicket was the Zimbabwean Noël Estcourt who was caught by Bob Broadbent for six. His second wicket was the better-known Robin Marlar, who was caught behind by George Mills (also making his debut) for two, and his third wicket was John Asquith who was caught by Broadbent for 12.*

*Worcestershire were dismissed for 89 (Jack Riley 1), with Thomas Hare taking 5-35.*

*Despite half-centuries from Dennis Silk (53) and West Indian Test cricketer Gerry Alexander – who was caught by Jack Riley off Roly Jenkins for 61 – Cambridge were dismissed for 194, with Jenkins claiming 5-73.*

*Needing 205 to win, Worcestershire achieved their target for the loss of three wickets, thanks mainly to 77 from Don Kenyon.*

Riley was raised in Clayton-le-Moors near Accrington and was educated locally at All Saints School. He played all his cricket in the Lancashire League, starting in Accrington's third XI before breaking into the first XI in 1949. His debut game was against Lowerhouse, who had in their side the West Indian Manny Martindale as their 'pro'. In spite of his presence Accrington won by four wickets.

From 1950 until he retired in 1968, Riley spent most of his career with Enfield, where he played over 300 matches, captaining them between 1956 and 1963. In 1954 and 1955 he was professional for Great Haywood Cricket Club, returning to Enfield thereafter.

In 1951 he took 40 wickets at an average of just 19.77, including five wickets in an innings on three occasions. His best figures were 6-54 in the six-wicket victory over Bacup. In the game against Nelson in May, Enfield were dismissed for just 38 with Indian Test cricketer Dattu Phadkar taking 8-21. The 'pro' in the Enfield side was Clyde Walcott and in a letter I received from Riley in 2002 he explained: *'I first met Clyde when he came to Enfield and we became firm friends. We stayed in touch and still do to this day. He's a great friend of mine.'*

On 19 July 1951 Riley had the honour to be selected for Clyde Walcott's Commonwealth XI in a game against Cumberland and Westmorland at the Ernest Valentine Ground in Workington. The star-studded side included Frank Worrell, Everton Weekes,

Roy Marshall and Sonny Ramadhin, and the highlight was 70 from Weekes and 72 from Walcott in a drawn game. Riley, though, went wicketless as his seven overs cost 28 runs.

*Riley as captain of Enfield CC.*

In 1952 Riley married Minnie Woolley at a service as Haslingden. They were to have three children, Philip, Christine and Susan. During that same summer Riley had another fine season, taking 34 wickets at an average of 16.61, with best figures of 8-46 in the three-wicket win against Ramsbottom at the Acre Bottom Ground in Ramsbottom.

Prior to making his first-class debut in 1953, Riley played for Worcestershire seconds against Warwickshire seconds at Seth Somers Park, Halesowen, which the visitors won by nine wickets thanks to Jack Bannister who finished with match figures of 10-61. Later in the month, having made his first-class debut, his final game of second-team cricket was against Gloucestershire at New Road in a 273-run victory. Dismissing Gloucestershire for 60 in their second innings, Martin Horton claimed 4-12 with Riley taking two wickets for a solitary run, delivering six overs, five of which were maidens.

Riley's profession was accountancy, something he chose as an alternative to cricket. In his letter to me he said: *'I enjoyed my short time at Worcester but didn't pursue it further as I wanted to pass my Association of Chartered Accountants qualification, which I did. Perhaps I might have had the same success with Worcestershire. Who knows?'*

He spent most his career at Walker Steel and rose to become chief executive officer. Walker Steel was a family business and became famous when it was sold in 1991 for a reported £360m, the then owner, Jack Walker, becoming the owner and benefactor of Blackburn Rovers Football Club who won the Premier League under his guidance.

*Enfield CC centenary celebration game.*
*Riley is seated fourth from the left.*

For Enfield Club's centenary in 1959 Riley played against a West Indies XI which included Conrad Hunte and Manny Martindale.

Another fine season followed in 1962, when he claimed 30 wickets at just 14.70 apiece with a best of 7-72 against Church in June. In August 1963 he proved the match winner in the game against Ramsbottom, when, in reply to Enfield's 133 all out, Ramsbottom were dismissed for 42 with Riley having the remarkable figures of 5-1 from 4.7 eight-ball overs.

The game was associated with a humorous story from the night before when Ramsbottom professional, 19-year-old Australian Ian Chappell, had gone from the pub to an Indian restaurant called The Khazi and then on to a club. At 3am he felt a tap on the shoulder.

*'Are you Ian Chappell?'* he was asked. The man with the query was the West Indian all-rounder Charlie Stayers.

Chappell: *'Er, yes.'*

Stayers: *'Am I pleased to see you. I'm Charlie Stayers, the pro for Enfield. I was a bit worried that you were home in bed getting an early night. That's terrific, let me buy you a drink!'*

Chappell was dismissed for 23 by Stayers who finished with 4-25.

In 1967 Riley finished the season with 23 wickets, his best performance of 6-32 coming in the game against Colne; however, chasing just 136 to win, Enfield fell short by 15 runs. The following season was to be his last, his tally of 14 wickets signalling that it was time to retire. In a League career spanning 19 years, he finished with 474 wickets which included 19 five-wicket hauls.

# ROGERS

**RUPERT ASHBY CAVE ROGERS (LATER KNOWN AS RUPERT ASHBY CAVE-ROGERS) – RIGHT-HAND BAT, OFF-BREAK BOWLER**

Born: Tixall, Staffordshire, 27 May 1902
Died: Eastbourne, Sussex, 2 May 1976

*Portrait of Rupert Rogers.*

First-class matches for Worcestershire: 1, versus Warwickshire, Edgbaston, Birmingham, 4 and 5 August 1919

Innings: 1; Not out: 0; Runs: 3; Highest score: 3; Caught: 1; Wickets: 0; Best bowling: 0-25

*Match drawn. This two-day fixture was played as a friendly – as were all of Worcestershire's games in 1919 – however, the matches were afforded first-class status. In their first-innings total of 330, Worcestershire were indebted to 'Dick' Burrows with 82 and Wing Commander William Shakespeare with 62. Rogers, batting at three, contributed just three runs before being caught and bowled by Albert Howell.*

*Warwickshire replied with 391-9 declared, with debutant Horace Venn scoring 151 before being caught by Rogers. Worcestershire closed their second innings on 162-0, with Alfred Cliff 81 not out and Wing Commander Shakespeare 67 not out.*

*Herbert Isaac was also making his debut in this game and features elsewhere in this publication.*

There has been conjecture for a long time over whether Rupert's correct surname is Rogers or Cave-Rogers? When he was born, he was given three 'first' names, Rupert, Ashby and Cave, with Rogers being his surname. His birth certificate shows Rupert Ashby C Rogers and there is no evidence to show he was baptised or christened. Throughout the majority of his career he was known as Rupert Rogers, with the hyphenated Cave-Rogers being added in later life.

He was the son of Robert Cave Rogers (a brewer) and Dorothy Violet Ashby. His father was a fine cricketer who played for Cannock Town and Rugeley. He was also a founder member of Staffordshire Gentlemen, whom he represented for over 30 years. On his retirement, he was presented with a silver salver as a thank you for his dedication to the Club, thereafter spending his retirement living in Somerset.

Rupert Rogers was educated at Malvern College where, between June 1918 and June 1919, he played for the cricket first XI and on 8 June 1918 starred with the bat scoring 44 in the drawn game with Shrewsbury School. The outstanding player in the side was Malvern's captain Norman Partridge, who played with Rogers during the same 12-month period, taking eight five-wicket hauls and scoring four centuries, including 229 not out against Repton School. He was to represent Warwickshire between 1921 and 1937, for whom he took 393 career wickets and scored one first-class hundred.

THE GENTLEMEN OF STAFFORDSHIRE'S XI

Seated : Colonel C. Hatton, Captain Cave-Rogers, E. W. Page, B. Meakin and J. B. Russell.   Standing : J. F. Scott, G. Mackarness, W. H. Adams, W. M. Tonkinson, B. McCall, G. H. Thorneycroft.

*Gentlemen of Staffordshire XI. Robert Cave-Rogers is seated, second from the left.*

The year 1919 saw Rogers play in his sole first-class game for Worcestershire and in doing so he became their fourth-youngest player aged 17 years and 69 days.

Rogers also played 11 football matches for Corinthians FC. After the War the Corinthians 'A' Team played games against school sides each November as they undertook their public schools' tour with annual fixtures against Repton, Malvern and Shrewsbury. Rogers appeared in four tours from 1919 until 1922, the highlight coming in the game against Malvern on 8 November 1919. Playing at outside left he scored twice, with fellow Worcestershire cricketers G.N. Foster (with a hat-trick) and W.W. Lowe (with one goal) completing the scoring. Foster was also secretary to the Corinthians FC team which merged with Corinthian Casuals to form The Casuals in 1939.

Rogers 'went up' to Cambridge and during his three years there became a leading figure with the Footlights, successfully producing its Club Revue show each year.

His involvement with the Footlights heralded the beginning of a long and successful life in acting, musical comedy and production. He began his career as understudy to Billy Leonard in *Patricia* at His Majesty's Theatre, London in 1924, and for two years appeared in *Midnight Follies* at the Hotel Metropole. He worked alongside big names such as Jack Buchanan and Gertrude Lawrence and subsequently understudied for Fred Astaire in *Lady be Good* at The Empire, Leicester Square.

In his first tour he played Astaire's part in *Lady be Good* but had to relinquish it due to a cartilage injury (which necessitated surgery) sustained while dancing on stage. He also played in the musical comedies *No, No, Nanette, Lady Mary* and *So This is Love*. Another successful appearance was with Sonnie Hale and Jessie Matthews in C.B. Cochran's *Wake Up and Dream* revue.

Continuing to tour, he was making headlines for all the right reasons. 'Stafford Artiste in Next Week's Play' was used by the local press to promote his appearance in what was described as the '*brilliant*' musical comedy, *The Girl Friend* at Wolverhampton's Grand Theatre. He had appeared previously in the same show at the Palace Theatre, London, which had also met with great acclaim.

Despite his busy schedule, Rogers found time to play cricket and in June 1927, played for Staffordshire Gentlemen against Derbyshire Friars at the County Ground, Derby. He only managed two runs, though, as the Friars won by 90 runs. The report of the game appeared below the County Championship table which made for disappointing reading. Worcestershire were bottom with just one win and nine defeats from their opening 10 games. They remained bottom, as they had in 1926, and were to do so for a third consecutive season in 1928.

Rogers married Miriam Mary Hoare-Ward on 27 June 1928, at Christ Church, Brondesbury in Middlesex. It was reported in the *Eastbourne Gazette* that the ceremony took place quietly, 'due to professional reasons' which were undisclosed.

The Gloucester public made the acquaintance of Rupert Cave-Rogers last year through his production of "No, No, Nanette," and this in itself is a testimony to his ability as a producer of the highest class.

Mr. Cave-Rogers appeared at home and abroad in the original production, and Caer Glow feel confident that under his skilful—sometimes even a trifle strict—guidance, once more Gloucester audiences will be assured of a well-produced modern show.

*Programme from The Girl Friend in 1935.*

Concentrating more on production, Rogers initially worked with Stafford Operatic Society and then on short-term contracts with leading amateur dramatic societies across the country.

In October 1935 he produced *The Girl Friend* for the Caer Glow Amateur Operatic and Dramatic Society, at the Shire Hall in Gloucester. He continued with shows at other venues, including the Borough Hall in Stafford and Victoria Hall, Hanley.

In the late-1930s he began a long association with the Eastbourne-based touring variety show *Twinkle*, run by Clarkson Rose and his wife Olive Fox. The show played a big role in the later part of Rogers's career and was described in the *Radio Times* as '*the standard by which all other musical shows are judged*'. Performances continued during the War, with *Twinkle* frequently appearing on the BBC Home Service.

*The* Eastbourne Herald *promoting the Twinkle show on 31 August, 1940.*

Twinkle *in its heyday – Rogers enjoying cricket at The Saffrons in Eastbourne. He is seated second from the left.*

*Twinkle* was popular at seaside resorts around the country after first appearing at Ryde Pier in 1921. It toured and did summer seasons for the next 45 years but by the mid-1960s, its demise was evident when end-of-the-pier shows were in decline. In the *Eastbourne Gazette* in 1963, Olive Fox summed up the situation and stated that: '*nobody wants to book us this year*'.

Rogers remained in Eastbourne where he retired and subsequently died in 1976.

# RUDGE

## LLOYD MAURICE RUDGE – RIGHT-HAND BAT, RIGHT-ARM FAST

Born: Walsall, Staffordshire, 11 February 1934
Died: Worcester, 15 October 1990

*Portrait of Lloyd Rudge.*

First-class matches for Worcestershire: 1 versus Combined Services, New Road, Worcester, 4, 5, 6 June 1952

Innings: 1; Not out: 0; Runs: 1; Highest score: 1; Caught: 0; Wickets: 0; Best bowling: 0-36

*Match drawn. Batting first, Worcestershire were dismissed for 229, with only Laddie Outschoorn (68) making a score of note. Lloyd Rudge's contribution was a single before being run out.*

*In reply, the Combined Services amassed 548-4 declared with centuries from David Heath (149), John Manners (103) and Jim Parks (103 not out). For good measure, there were half-centuries from Alan Shirreff (54) and Robert Wilson (67). Lloyd Rudge bowled 12 overs for 36 runs.*

*Worcestershire closed their second innings on 168-3, with half-centuries from Don Kenyon (51) and Outschoorn (54) as the game ended in a draw. John Spilsbury was also making his debut for Worcestershire in this game and features elsewhere in this publication.*

Although born in Walsall, Lloyd Rudge grew up in Worcester, living in Cope Road with his mother Margaret and his father Francis, who was a butcher.

He attended Samuel Southall School (known locally as Sammy's) where his talent as a football centre-forward and as a fast bowler shone through to the extent that Worcestershire showed an interest in him from an early age. He was coached by Worcestershire's legendary fast bowler Reg Perks, who developed the skills of his apprentice to the extent that he was regarded as 'the next Reg Perks'.

On leaving school aged 15, Rudge embarked on an apprenticeship with Archdale Engineering in Worcester as a machine tool fitter. During this time he had trials to join the nursery team at Worcestershire but, with his apprenticeship and future finances in mind, could not commit to being a full-time player. He was, however, still taken on the nursery staff.

'I have a trade' was his mantra, and so he continued to play mainly for Archdale's. It was while trialling at Worcester as an eighteen-year-old that he made his first-class appearance in early June 1952, in the drawn game with Combined Services. There were six Worcestershire players and triallists under the age of 21 in the side.

Later that month, he found himself back playing for the Club and Ground XI, taking 2-18 in the low-scoring defeat to King's School.

In 1955 Rudge began his national service in the RAF where, having completed his service, he chose to stay for an additional six months so that he could continue to play sport for them.

He then returned to Archdale's where he enjoyed participating in their strong sports and social club activities, representing many of their different sides. They were so strong that they were able to field two sides for virtually every sport they decided to participate in. A regular fixture was the annual cricket match against the touring team Surrey Optimists.

In June 1958 Rudge took 8-9, including a hat-trick in a game against Kalamazoo, who were bowled out for 23 in response to Archdale's 163-8 declared. The local *Sports Argus* reported that *'Kalamazoo found the pace of L Rudge too much to handle.'*

*Advertisement for James Archdale and Company.*

In July 1959 Rudge married Cynthia Skidmore and continued to work for Archdale's until it closed in 1968. The company had been founded in Birmingham by James Archdale 100 years earlier and had moved to a factory in Blackpole, Worcester after World War Two.

For several seasons Rudge was the leading wicket-taker and frequently won the bowling cup for outstanding performances in the works' league. Following the closure of Archdale's he continued in the same line of work, firstly with K.R. Matthews at Diglis in Worcester and then Darius Engineers in Droitwich.

He maintained his love of sports, mainly cricket and football, but was also keen on his pub games, especially dominoes, cards and skittles. He died suddenly in 1990 in the house in which he had lived all his married life and where his wife Cynthia still lives today.

# RUTHERFORD

**IAN ALEXANDER RUTHERFORD – RIGHT-HAND BAT, RIGHT-ARM OFF-BREAK/RIGHT-ARM MEDIUM**

Born: Dunedin, Otago, New Zealand, 30 June 1957

*Portrait of Ian Rutherford in 2020.*

First-class matches for Worcestershire: 2
- – versus Oxford University, The Parks, Oxford, 26, 27, 28 May 1976
- – versus West Indians, New Road, Worcester, 18, 19, 20 August 1976

Innings: 3; Not out: 0; Runs: 9; Highest score: 8; Caught: 1; Wickets: 1; Best bowling: 1-15

*Against Oxford University, Worcestershire won by eight wickets. Winning the toss and fielding, Worcestershire dismissed Oxford for 94 with Paul Pridgeon taking 7-35. Worcestershire declared on 341-7 with centuries from Ted Hemsley (157) and Dipak Patel (100 not out). In this game, Patel became the youngest Worcestershire player to score a first-class hundred aged 17 years and 215 days. Rutherford was stumped by Paul Fisher (who played for Worcestershire between 1980 and 1981) off the bowling of Andrew Wingfield Digby without score.*

*Dismissing the students for 330 (Vic Marks 105) and (Simon Clements 50), Worcestershire were set 84 to win which they achieved for the loss of two wickets, with Alan Ormrod finishing unbeaten on 55.*

*Against the West Indians, the visitors won by eight wickets. Winning the toss and batting, Worcestershire were dismissed for 358 with Rutherford (who opened the innings) scoring eight before being caught by Clive Lloyd off Michael Holding. Phil Neale made 143, his maiden first-class century, and there were half-centuries for Dipak Patel (51) and Basil D'Oliveira (60).*

*The tourists replied with 408 thanks to 109 from Collis King (who played for Worcestershire in 1983) and half-centuries from Roy Fredericks (53), Viv Richards (57) and Clive Lloyd (73). In just 40.5 overs Worcestershire were dismissed in their second innings for 86, Rutherford falling lbw to Bernard Julien for a single.*

*The West Indians reached their target of 37 for the loss of two wickets, one of which fell to Rutherford. Wicket-keeper Mike Findlay was caught by Barry Jones for 10.*

Rutherford first played representative cricket for Otago under-20s in December 1971 and made his debut for them in first-class cricket in a Plunket Shield game against Canterbury, starting on Boxing Day 1974. Scores of 29 and 46 made for a promising start. His opening partner was Otago captain Glenn Turner, who also played for Worcestershire from 1967 until 1982 and is rated as one of the finest batsmen to have ever represented the County.

Rutherford's maiden first-class hundred came in the game against Central Districts at Cook's Gardens, Wanganui, in January

1976, when he reached 121 in the second innings of the drawn game. Following a brief spell with Central Districts in the middle of the 1977–78 season, he returned to Otago where he remained until the end of the 1983–84 season.

With Turner having an influence on his decision to join Worcestershire in 1976, Rutherford played for both the Club and Ground XI and the second XI. He made further appearances in the Warwick Pool under-25 competition, with a best performance of 111 not out against Warwickshire in the game played at the Birmingham University Ground in Redditch.

He was joined in the seconds for part of the season by fellow countryman Warren Lees, who went on to play 21 Test matches for New Zealand.

Rutherford had an outstanding 1976 for the seconds. In 17 games he scored 1,158 runs at an average of 36.18 and hit three centuries, his best being 117 versus Nottinghamshire at Tipton Road, Dudley, in late-August. He enjoyed playing alongside good friends Dipak Patel and Barry Jones. The three of them are seen here having received their second XI caps. Rutherford is in the centre.

*Rutherford wearing his second XI cap.*

Rutherford played in the early-season fixture against Oxford University and his consistent form throughout the summer led to his introduction to the first team in a game against the powerful West Indian touring side.

*Rutherford opening the innings against the West Indians.*

In February 1977 Rutherford opened for Otago with Stu McCullum (father of Brendon and Nathan) in the game against the touring Australians. Requiring 267 to win they shared an opening partnership of 126, with Rutherford scoring 52 and McCullum 75. Disappointingly, though, the team fell short by 48 runs as Ray Bright took 5-53.

By now, Rutherford was studying accountancy at Otago University in Dunedin and later qualified with a bachelor of commerce degree in 1979. Then, after training as a chartered accountant, he became a Member of the New Zealand Society of Accountants in 1981.

In the final of the Shell Trophy, in March 1979, he scored 222 in the game against Central Districts. Despite it being a drawn game, Otago won on first innings having amassed 543-8 declared to which Central Districts replied with 275. In an e-mail I received, Rutherford referred to this innings as the highlight of his career: *'This was a special moment for me. Both my brother Ken and nephew Hamish – who have both played for New Zealand – have also scored over 200 in an innings for Otago at first-class level, which is a rare occurrence.'* Like his uncle before him, Hamish has also played for Worcestershire, scoring a century on his first-class debut for them (123) in the Championship game against Leicestershire at Grace Road in 2019.

In March 1980, Rutherford played three games for Young New Zealand and in the third match scored 75 against D.H. Robins' XI for whom Dipak Patel scored 105.

Rutherford continued to play for Otago until he retired at the end of the 1983–84 season. After his exploits of 1979 the volume of runs began to reduce and he scored just seven further half-centuries during that time. His best was 96 in the innings and 87-run victory against Canterbury at Queen's Park, Invercargill, in January 1983. In 1984 he had the satisfaction of playing in the same Otago side as his brother Ken, the game against Canterbury ending in a five-wicket defeat for Otago.

Rutherford returned to his former profession, working for a chartered accountancy firm for six years before setting up in practice of his own in 1987, which he still runs today.

While he is not currently involved in cricket he has played a variety of roles in the recent past, including coaching, administration, selecting and managing players from schoolboy level through to the first-class game.

He has been living in Alexandra in Central Otago for the last 40 years and is near-neighbours with Glenn Turner who lives in

Wanaka and Warren Lees in Clyde. He enjoys his golf, playing off a handicap of 14, and is a vice-president of Alexandra Golf Club. He enjoys many sports but his other main passion is horse racing, and he has interests in a number of racing syndicates.

# SCOTHERN

## MICHAEL GRAEME SCOTHERN – RIGHT-HAND BAT, RIGHT-ARM FAST-MEDIUM

Born: Skipton, Yorkshire, 9 March 1961

*Mike Scothern in 2020.*

First-class matches for Worcestershire: 1 versus Cambridge University, Fenner's, 12, 13, 14 June 1985

Innings: Did not bat; Caught: 0; Wickets: 1; Best bowling: 1-42

*Match drawn. While Worcestershire entertained Zimbabwe at New Road, seven players were given first-class debuts in the match at Cambridge. Three of them – Lawrence Smith, Stuart Lampitt and Paul Bent – all subsequently played Championship cricket. Four of them – Mike Scothern along with Harshad Patel, Mel Hussain and Brian Barrett, who feature elsewhere in this publication – were not afforded the same opportunity.*

*Thanks to half-centuries from acting captain and wicket-keeper David Humphries (62 not out) and David Banks (50 not out) a crisis was averted and Worcestershire posted 216-5 declared. Due to bad weather the University replied with 143-6. Scothern bowled 16 overs and claimed one wicket.*

Scothern was educated at Ermysteds Grammar School in Skipton and having completed his A levels, spent five years working for Barclays Bank and playing in their Leeds District cricket team. While playing for them he told me: *'It was then that I decided that I could give cricket a go, and after trial nets and a game, I was given a trialist period at Worcestershire towards the back half of one season and the front half of the following season.'*

The games to which Scothern refers are two second XI games in August 1984. His debut was in the match against Derbyshire at Shipley where he picked up the wicket of future England Test left-armer Paul Taylor. A young Graeme Hick was also making his way with Worcestershire and plundered 170; a fortnight later in the game against Leicestershire at Grace Road, Hick followed up with 186, with Scothern picking up one wicket.

In May 1985 Scothern picked up six further wickets for the seconds in the game against Glamorgan at New Road, including 4-60 in the second innings (and the wicket of future England opener Steve James) as Worcestershire won by an innings and 62. Hick was the star of the show once more, striking 187. Scothern commented: *'I really enjoyed my time at the County. I was there as Graeme Hick developed into a world-class player. It was wonderful to see him bat the way he did.'*

The following month Scothern made his first-class debut against Cambridge University in a game ruined by bad weather. He did, however, have time to claim his sole first-class wicket, that of future England rugby captain Rob Andrew, the England fly half, whom he had lbw for two.

He played one further second XI game that season before leaving the Club and said: *'I did pretty well, but the weather turned really bad that summer and the coach – Basil D'Oliveira, who was a really nice man – released me because the contracted players were not getting enough of a game. That was very disappointing.'*

The consolation for Scothern was that his club side, Barnoldswick (known as 'Barlick'), had a fantastic season and were crowned League champions, Ramsbottom Cup winners and Craven Cup winners.

*The 'Barlick' team from 1985. Scothern is standing,*
*second from the right.*

Scothern then embarked on a 13-year career with Cumberland in the Minor Counties Championship, his best season being 1994 when he took 33 wickets, including three five-wicket hauls. His best was 6-53 against Buckinghamshire at Tynefield Park in Penrith.

In 1986, Cumberland beat Oxfordshire in the Minor Counties Championship Final at New Road, Worcester. Scothern claimed 2-32 from his 11 overs as Cumberland won by two wickets, a victory he describes as one of his career highlights.

*Cumberland, 1986 Minor Counties Champions –*
*Scothern is on the front row, second from the left.*

By now, Scothern was working for the family business, Harry Garlick, an electrical retailer. His father began working for the company in 1953, ultimately becoming a partner and taking over the business in the early 1970s. Specialising in consumer electronics, Scothern continues his involvement and is now company director, with responsibility for eight stores across the north of England. The company employs 60 people.

Scothern recalled some of his other memories in cricket, from Nat West Trophy games against Worcestershire. The first game was in 1988: *'It was always good to go back to New Road and although we were thrashed – and my 12 overs went for 93 – it was another magnificent innings from Graeme Hick which stands out in my mind; he got 138. In 1995, though, we gave them a real fright. We had them 81-4 off 30 overs with both Hick and Moody back in the pavilion. I picked up the wicket of Tim Curtis but Gavin Haynes with 116 not out rescued them. We closed on 192-9 from our 60 overs and I managed to pick up 18 in the run chase, but we lost by 65 runs.'*

The same season he represented the Minor Counties in a Benson and Hedges Cup game against Durham and recalled being on the wrong side of a 'Nedding'. – Ned being a nickname for Wayne Larkins - who scored 123 as Durham won by just seven runs.

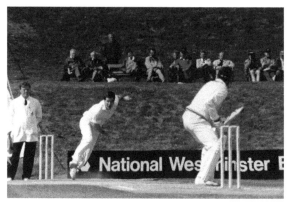

*Scothern in action during the Nat West game for Cumberland against Leicestershire at Kendal in 1994.*

In June the following year he finished with career-best figures in the Nat West Trophy, when he picked up 3-29 from his 11 overs in the 102-run defeat to Middlesex.

In each of the three seasons from 2001 to 2003 Scothern took a hat-trick for 'Barlick'. The third one came in a tight game against Read CC, who, needing 140 to win, found themselves on 137-7, with former Australian Test cricketer Peter Sleep going well on 70. Stranded at the non-striker's end, Sleep could only watch as Scothern – known for bowling straight – took the last three wickets, all lbw to claim an unlikely victory.

Scothern's proudest League moment came in 2013 when he captained the Ribblesdale League team to their only ever win in the Manchester Evening News Inter League competition, beating a very strong Bolton League team in the final.

He is still involved with 'Barlick', helps coach the juniors and is Club secretary. He retired from playing three years ago to concentrate on triathlon and has now completed three Ironman triathlons, an achievement he is especially proud of.

*Scothern completing an Ironman triathlon.*

Despite thinking that his cricket career was over, Scothern was persuaded out of retirement in 2019 to play for Yorkshire over-60s, as an underage player for the 2020 season. He was eligible as he was still only 59 at the time of his selection.

# SHEPPARD

### GEOFFREY ALLAN SHEPPARD – BATTING UNKNOWN, BOWLING UNKNOWN

Born: Ibstock, Leicestershire, 18 December 1890
Died: Henwick, Newbury, Berkshire, 22 May 1940

*Portrait of Geoffrey Sheppard.*

First-class matches for Worcestershire: 2
- Versus Gloucestershire, New Road, Worcester, 23, 24 June 1919
- Versus Somerset, New Road Worcester, 7, 8 July 1919

Innings: 4; Not out: 0; Runs: 18; Highest score: 11; Caught: 2; Did not bowl

*Against Gloucestershire, match drawn. Batting first, Worcestershire were dismissed for 201 with a half-century for Thomas Allchurch (51). Sheppard made 11 before becoming one of Francis Ellis's four victims.*

215

*Gloucestershire replied with 334, thanks to contributions from Harry Huggins (92), Philip Williams (59) and Harry Smith (74). In their second innings Worcestershire declared on 282-9 with half-centuries from Cecil Turner (72), Fred Bowley (50) and Maurice Jewell (84). This set Gloucestershire 150 to win. They closed on 109-4 with Foster Robinson contributing 62.*

*Cecil Tipper was also making his debut in this game and features elsewhere in this publication.*

*Against Somerset, match drawn. In response to Somerset's 172, Worcestershire replied with 203 thanks to 101 from Fred Bowley. Batting at number eight Sheppard was bowled by Jim Bridges without scoring.*

*In their second innings Somerset were dismissed for 240, with Sydney Rippon (73) and Philip Hope (54) holding the innings together. Requiring 210 to win, Worcestershire held on for the draw closing on 149-8 thanks to a second half-century from Bowley (50). Sheppard was caught and bowled for two by Jack 'Farmer' White.*

Geoffrey Sheppard's parents, Catherine and William Philpott Sheppard – he a colliery proprietor – lived at Ibstock House in Leicestershire. It was in Ibstock where Geoffrey was baptised on 22 February 1891. He had two older brothers, Samuel, who was born in 1884, and John, who was born in 1888.

Sheppard was educated at Charterhouse between 1905 and 1909. He was a member of 'Gownboys' House for which he played cricket, football and pairs rackets. He did not play cricket for the first XI but his brother John did achieve that milestone.

In 1910 Sheppard matriculated at Trinity Hall, Cambridge and obtained a bachelor of arts by proxy in 1915. He was registered as an affiliated student and was allowed special examination on account of his military service. While at Cambridge, he played cricket, football and hockey for his college.

*Portrait of Sheppard taken at Trinity Hall, Cambridge.*

The *Silver Crescent* – Trinity's student magazine – provides an insight into Sheppard's early life, his time at University and what he was like as a man: *'Known by the nickname "Bush", he is six foot, six inches tall and is recognised by his great shoulders rounded in a veritable "scholar's stoop", along with a long, thin pipe steaming in his mouth.*

'He was captain of his cricket team at his private school and then in 1905 joined Charterhouse. He played football, cricket, hockey and rackets but it was not until he came up to The Hall in 1910, after a year's cramming, that he really distinguished himself. In rapid succession he won Crescents for cricket, hockey and football and in his second year was elected to the Crescent Club. He is now captain of both hockey and cricket clubs and is regarded as one of the mainstays of Hall field sports.

'But "Bush" is endowed with extraordinary versatility. In addition to his athletic achievements he has passed the "Little-Go", won a silver cup for the Varsity Open Motor Cycling Handicap at Brooklands, has been a prominent figure in the "Owls" and is a private in the Officer Training Corps. He is going for the Army and is engaged in absorbing military knowledge for the War Office examination.*

217

*'Bush's motto – so he says – is "work before all" and we feel sure that his innate industry, coupled with his characteristics of a "man of blood and iron" is bound to carry him far in life.'*

In 1913, while still at Trinity Hall, Sheppard enrolled with the Isaac Newton Freemasons Lodge, yet just 12 months later was serving as a second lieutenant in the 2nd Battalion of the Worcestershire Regiment after War broke out. He was to witness some of the fiercest fighting of the War.

*Captain Sheppard.*

In October 1914, the outcome of the Battle of Ypres hinged around the village of Gheluvelt, which had been lost, meaning that a serious gap had been made in the British line. Unless the gap could be closed, a breakthrough could not be avoided.

On the evening 30 October the Second Battalion remained uncommitted, all other units having been sent to reinforce the line. Located in Polygon Wood, the Battalion received an order to attack and retake Gheluvelt. Amid the chaos they moved from the Wood towards the Chateau which dominated the village. They alone were moving towards the enemy, Major Hankey deciding that the only way to cross the dangerous area was at the double, in order to face the enemy head on.

Gheluvelt was saved and the line restored. The Worcestershire Regiment records state: *'It is rare that the action of one unit can exert such a profound influence as did this now famous counter-attack.'* Sheppard had survived, but 187 of his comrades had perished; his resolve as a 'man of blood and iron' had been tested to the full.

*The Gheluvelt survivors - taken in 1926.*
*Captain Sheppard is seated in the middle.*

By the time the War concluded Sheppard had been promoted to the rank of captain and in 1919 he made his two first-class appearances for Worcestershire. On leave from the Army, he played occasional games of cricket and in July 1929 played for the Gentlemen of Worcestershire against Bromsgrove School in a drawn game. The highlight was 117 from the stylish Cyril Walters, who went on to captain Worcestershire and play 11 Test matches for England.

Later in the season Sheppard toured with the Gentleman of Worcestershire to the Channel Islands. He toured with them once more, to Denmark in 1930.

*Gentlemen of Worcestershire in Denmark, 1930. Sheppard is on the*
*back row, second from the left.*

In 1931 he appeared for the Butterflies and played four matches during a week-long tour of Kent, playing alongside his brother, John, and Hon. Charles Lyttelton, who was to captain Worcestershire from 1936 until 1939.

*Wedding of Geoffrey Sheppard and Susan Hemsted.*

By now Sheppard was living in Newbury, Berkshire, and in December 1935 married Susan Hemsted, the wedding making the society pages of the newspapers. They remained in Newbury until he died five years later, aged just 49.

In 1944 Susan married Henry Billington, a Wiltshire farmer and an international tennis player. She herself was a member of a celebrated British tennis dynasty: the former British number one Tim Henman was her grandson and she was a Wimbledon player in her own right.

Her mother, Ellen Stawell-Brown, competed at Wimbledon at the turn of the 20th century and in 1901 was reputedly the first woman to serve overarm. Susan Billington, on the other hand, was the last woman to serve underarm at the All England Lawn Tennis Club; she appeared regularly at Wimbledon in the 1950s, reaching the third round of the ladies' doubles in 1951, 1955 and 1956.

She saw service in the World War Two, driving Army staff cars and gravel lorries involved in the construction of Greenham Common aerodrome. She lived and farmed at The Creek in Henwick, where she helped raise a herd of Aberdeen Angus cattle and ran a small thoroughbred stud.

Both Susan and Henry Billington competed at Wimbledon, and regularly partnered each other in mixed doubles on Centre Court; Henry Billington appeared in the third round of the Davis Cup three times, in 1948, 1950 and 1951. As well as being a first-class tennis player, Susan Billington represented Berkshire at badminton and squash. She died in 2006.

# SHEPPARD

### THOMAS WINTER SHEPPARD – CHANGED TO THOMAS WINTER SHEPPARD-GRAHAM IN 1919. RIGHT-HAND BAT

Born: Emsworth, Hampshire, 4 March 1873
Died: Callander, Perthshire, 7 June 1954

*Portrait of Thomas Sheppard.*

First-class matches for Worcestershire: 1 versus Oxford University, The Parks, Oxford, 17, 18, 19 June 1909

Innings: 2; Not out: 0; Runs: 36; Highest score: 22; Caught: 0; Did not bowl

*Oxford University won by 42 runs. Winning the toss and batting, Oxford scored 213 thanks to Malcolm Salter (58) and Ronald Lagden (55). In reply, Worcestershire were dismissed for 163, with Sheppard – batting at number eight – scoring a creditworthy 22. Roy Robinson with 5-75 was the pick of the bowlers.*

*Thanks to 102 from Charles Hooman, the students made 239 leaving Worcestershire needing 290 to win. They were dismissed for 247 with only John Cuffe (88) making a contribution of note. Sheppard was bowled by Frederick Turner for 14. Jack Barley was*

*also making his debut for Worcestershire in this game and appears elsewhere in this publication.*

Sheppard's father, Major Thomas Winter Sheppard (who played cricket for the Gibraltar Garrison in 1858), died before his son was born. His wife re-married; however, it was Thomas's grandfather, Henry Winter Sheppard, who brought him up and played a significant part in his life.

On leaving school, Thomas Jnr went to the Royal Academy at Sandhurst and subsequently became a career soldier. On 25 February 1893 he joined the King's Liverpool Regiment as a second lieutenant just before his 20th birthday.

He was promoted to lieutenant on 20 September 1895 and captain on 21 March 1900, before travelling to South Africa for the second Boer War where he served with the Mounted Infantry. He remained there until 1902 and on his return was transferred to the 12th Provisional Battalion.

*Sheppard in army uniform.*

On 26 April 1905 he married Violet Mary Morgan (her pet name was Tommy) at Rye in Sussex. They had three children: Frederick born in 1906, Cecilia Margaret born in 1908 and Roland Frank born in 1915.

In August 1905 he made his Championship debut playing for Hampshire in the game against Yorkshire at The Circle in Hull. In a drawn game, batting at number four, he was dismissed by the great George Hirst for 17.

In a three-day game starting on 14 May 1906 he represented the Army in a match against Hampshire played at the Officers Club Services Ground in Aldershot, being dismissed for scores of nought and one.

Three months later he scored 116, hitting 18 boundaries before retiring hurt in a game for MCC against the Public Schools at Lord's. The report in the *London Standard* described the Public Schools' batting and bowling as *'feeble'* and their fielding as *'deplorably slack'*, as Sheppard and his partner, Eric Smith, took the score past 170 in just over an hour's play. He continued to play for MCC until 1913.

In both 1907 and 1908, Sheppard played for the Free Foresters against Oxford University, top-scoring in the second game with 37 as Oxford won by 107 runs. He also represented the Army against the Royal Navy at Lord's in June 1908 and was a key figure in instigating the game as an annual fixture. On this occasion, he failed to trouble the scorers as the game finished in a draw. The following season, he made his sole first-class appearance for Worcestershire, who were defeated by Oxford University. Between 1910 and 1912 he played for Liverpool in the Liverpool District Competition.

After promotion to captain in 1912 Sheppard served with the 8th Foot, King's Liverpool Regiment during World War One. He was wounded and spent time recovering at Mrs Watney's Nursing

Home for Officers at Charles Street in Mayfair, which entitled him to wear the 'wound stripe'.

In 1915 he was promoted to major and in 1918 was mentioned in despatches for 'distinguished and gallant services', He was promoted, temporarily, to lieutenant-colonel. His medal index card from 1919 shows that he was awarded the 1914 Victory Medal with both 'clasp and roses' and in 1919 the Italian military decoration – the Croce al Merito di Guerra (the War Merit Cross) – which was instituted by King Victor Emmanuel III.

*Portrait of Major Sheppard.*

In 1919, Sheppard added the surname 'Graham' to his name when he inherited the Duchray and Rednock Estate from his uncle, the Reverend Henry Alexander Graham Sheppard. This prompted him to leave the Army and move to Scotland to live in Rednock House and manage the estate.

He was a keen follower of country pursuits and in his diaries from 1921 to 1951 he talks at length about hunting and fishing trips. He refers to the best methods of catching fish and other quarry and in some places pins fish hooks to the pages to demonstrate the flies he used while angling. He also made detailed instructions as to how these should be used.

He had a keen interest in current affairs along with a sound understanding of national and international politics, and had firm views on both military and political matters which were informed by his own experiences in two conflicts.

On 6 March 1929 his great nephew, David Stuart Sheppard, was born. David had a distinguished cricketing career with Cambridge University and Sussex and played 22 Tests for England. As the Right Reverend David Sheppard he became Lord Sheppard of Liverpool.

In April 1937, Thomas Sheppard was appointed deputy lieutenant of the county of Stirling and, as the likelihood of War loomed larger, his promotion to lieutenant-colonel was made permanent.

In his diary he refers to the 25 child evacuees from Glasgow whom he agreed to take in following the start of the War in September 1939. The youngsters lived in Rednock House and were looked after by his wife and daughter – Violet and Cecilia – and his housekeeper.

During the War he helped to organise the Air Raid Precaution in Port Menteith (where Rednock House was) and served as a volunteer warden. He also volunteered to work in the conscription office where he interviewed men set to join the Army.

*Formal portrait of Thomas Sheppard.*

# SPENCER

## HARRY NORMAN ERNEST SPENCER – RIGHT-HAND BAT, RIGHT-ARM MEDIUM

Born: Shipston-on-Stour, Warwickshire, 1 October 1901
Died: Hammersmith, London, 13 August 1954

*Harry Spencer in 1930.*

First-Class matches for Worcestershire: 1 versus The New Zealanders, New Road Worcester, 8, 9, 10 June 1927

Innings: 2; Not out: 0; Runs: 28; Highest score: 26; Caught: 2; Wickets: 2; Best bowling: 1-34

*The New Zealanders won by 194 runs. Winning the toss and batting, the The New Zealanders were dismissed for 276, with half-centuries for Ces Dacre (82) and captain Tom Lowry, who was bowled by Spencer for 74. 'Percy' Tarbox was the pick of the bowlers taking 6-88.*

*Worcestershire were dismissed for 222 with only Vic Fox (79) making runs of any consequence. Spencer was bowled by Bill Merritt for 26.*

*A score of 140 not out from 'Curly' Page and 106 from Lowry – who was caught and bowled by Spencer – allowed the visitors to declare on 349-5, leaving Worcestershire an unlikely 404 runs to win.*

*They were dismissed for 209 and were indebted to Fox once more for his 79. Spencer was bowled by Herb McGirr for two, leaving the New Zealanders victorious.*

From Warwickshire, the Spencer family owned Leasowes Farm at Radford Semele near Leamington. Harry Spencer was educated at King Edward VI School in Stratford-upon-Avon, where he shone at sport and during his last season at school took 50 wickets at less than four runs apiece.

On leaving school in 1917 he embarked on a career with Lloyds Bank for which he worked all his life. His first branch was in Stratford followed by six years at the Coventry branch before he returned to Stratford. He played League cricket for Stratford CC enjoying two spells with them, from 1919–1926 and 1931–1936. He also played rugby for Stratford and Kenilworth.

In 1923, while playing for Stratford, he took 3-52 in a one-wicket defeat to Warwickshire's Club and Ground XI. The connection with Warwickshire had been established, as two years later he represented their second XI in an eight-wicket victory over Derbyshire seconds at the Rutland Recreation Ground in Ilkeston.

After moving to Coventry and North Warwick CC in 1927 he had the opportunity to play for Worcestershire in June in his sole first-class game for them. He continued to play for Coventry and North Warwick until 1930; his best season was in 1929 when he took 80 wickets at nine runs each. He also 'guested' for Leamington during that time.

**OFFICIAL SCORE CARD.**

# Worcestershire County Cricket Club.

## WORCESTERSHIRE v. NEW ZEALAND.

JUNE 8th, 9th & 10th, 1927.    Umpires: Messrs. L. Braund & J. King.

### NEW ZEALAND.

| First innings. | | Second innings. | |
|---|---|---|---|
| 1  J. E. Mills lbw b Price | 2 | b Price | 34 |
| 2  K. C. James b Tarbox | 6 | lbw b Tarbox | 9 |
| 3  M. L. Page c Gibbons b Tarbox | 0 | not out | 140 |
| 4  T. C. Lowry b Spencer | 74 | c and b Spencer | 106 |
| 5  C. Allcott c Spencer b Tarbox | 35 | b Gibbons | 22 |
| 6  C. Oliver c Fox b Tarbox | 0 | not out | 20 |
| 7  C. C. Dacre b Tarbox | 82 | b Tarbox | 10 |
| 8  H. M. McGirr b Gibbons | 48 | | |
| 9  G. H. L. Bernau c Fox b Tarbox | 9 | | |
| 10  W. Merritt not out | 4 | | |
| 11  M. Henderson c Fox b Tarbox | 1 | | |
| Extras | 15 | Extras | 8 |
| Total | 276 | Total | 349* |

| Wickets | 1 | 2 | 3 | 4 | 5 | 6 | 7 | 8 | 9 | 10 |
|---|---|---|---|---|---|---|---|---|---|---|
| Runs | 3 | 4 | 11 | 116 | 117 | 140 | 255 | 263 | 275 | 276 |
| 2nd innings | 25 | 84 | 213 | 230 | 283 | | | | | |

\* Innings declared.

### WORCESTERSHIRE.

| | | | |
|---|---|---|---|
| 6  Wright lbw b Allcott | 7 | st James b Merritt | 2 |
| 10  King b Merritt | 18 | run out | 28 |
| 9  Gibbons b Allcott | 19 | lbw b Merritt | 17 |
| 8  Fox lbw b Merritt | 79 | c James b McGirr | 79 |
| 5  N. Spencer b Merritt | 26 | b McGirr | 2 |
| 7  Tarbox run out | 1 | c James b McGirr | 35 |
| 2  W. H. N. Shakespeare c Page b Henderson | 5 | b McGirr | 5 |
| 1  Hon. J. Coventry b Henderson | 7 | c Henderson b Allcott | 16 |
| 4  C. K. Foster not out | 16 | not out | 7 |
| 3  H. S. Garratt c Lowry b Merritt | 31 | c Mills b Merritt | 1 |
| 11  Price (J.) st James b Allcott | 4 | c Allcott b Merritt | 0 |
| Extras | 9 | Extras | 17 |
| Total | 222 | Total | 209 |

| Wickets | 1 | 2 | 3 | 4 | 5 | 6 | 7 | 8 | 9 | 10 |
|---|---|---|---|---|---|---|---|---|---|---|
| Runs | 13 | 37 | 67 | 117 | 126 | 161 | 170 | 175 | 210 | 222 |
| 2nd innings | 18 | 31 | 73 | 152 | 160 | 176 | 197 | 204 | 205 | 209 |

**For Latest Cricket Results and all Sports see**

# The Worcestershire Echo.

ALL LOVERS OF CRICKET SHOULD JOIN

## The Worcestershire County Cricket Club.

Subscriptions:—Gentlemen £1 11s. 6d.; Ladies £1 1s. 0d.; Family Tickets: £2 2s. 0d.,
£2 12s. 6d.; £3 3s. 0d.; Schoolboy Tickets 11/6; Season Tickets 10/- (admission to Ground only).
These can be obtained on application to the Secretary, County Ground.

H. C. Knott, Broad Street, Worcester.

*Scorecard from Worcestershire versus New Zealand, 1927.*

In 1928 Spencer played his first game for Warwickshire Imps, a side he was to occasionally play for over the next five seasons. In his last outing for the Imps (in 1933) against Bath he dismissed the great Somerset all-rounder Bertie Buse, but not before he had scored 105. In 1929, playing for Coventry and North Warwick against Warwickshire's Club and Ground XI, he scored 113 before he was out lbw to Cecil Tate, brother of the Sussex and England bowler Maurice Tate.

In 1929 he married Edna Hardy and they had a son, David. Her father, E.J. Hardy, was chairman of Birfield Industries Ltd, a large holding company that invented the famous Hardy Universal Joint which revolutionised the transport industry. The joint is still in worldwide use today. In 1966 Birfield Industries was taken over by **GKN (Guest Keen and Nettlefold) and today** GKN's Birfield joints command almost 50 per cent of global market share.

The first of Spencer's three Championship appearances for Warwickshire followed, all of them being in May 1930. Ironically, his debut match was against Worcestershire at Edgbaston. He bowled Worcestershire opener Leslie Wright for 16 with his very first delivery. He was, though, to remain wicketless in his next two Championship games. A return to the seconds yielded better results: against Derbyshire in June he scored 68 and picked up two wickets in the drawn game.

The remainder of his cricketing career was spent representing Lloyds Bank, which he captained, and Stratford again, where in 1933 he made 145 not out against Sutton Coldfield and 103 against Gloucester Bohemians.

He was a gifted golfer, playing off a handicap of two and representing both Warwickshire and Worcestershire, and was a medal winner at Stratford Golf Club in 1936 and 1937. During World War Two he was a special constable in Leamington, playing the occasional match for the police team.

From 1938 until 1945 Spencer was assistant manager of Lloyds Bank, Leamington, during which time, the family farming business was sold in 1944. He maintained his interest in farming and agriculture and was a member of the Warwickshire board of the National Farmers Union, the Royal Agricultural Society and the Shorthorn Society.

After being transferred on several previous occasions, Spencer's final move with Lloyds Bank was to Canterbury as branch manager. Embracing the bank's requirement to be involved in the local community, he was made a vice-president of Beverley Cricket Club in Canterbury and was connected to Canterbury Rugby Club and Canterbury Angling Society. He was honorary treasurer to a number of local organisations and continued his involvement as a senior freemason.

In June 1951 he played cricket once more, on this occasion for MCC against his old team, Coventry and North Warwick, in a game played at the Bulls Head Ground in Coventry. The MCC side contained no fewer than eight Worcestershire players who had played first-class cricket for the County, but the star of the show was Warwickshire's Jack Marshall, who top-scored with 103 before being run out.

Spencer became unwell in his early fifties. He was diagnosed with kidney failure and died in the Royal Masonic Hospital in Hammersmith in 1954.

# SPILSBURY

## JOHN WILLIAM EDWARD SPILSBURY – RIGHT-HAND BAT, RIGHT-ARM FAST

Born: Worcester, 27 October 1933

*Portrait of John Spilsbury.*

First-class matches for Worcestershire: 1 versus Combined Services, New Road, Worcester, 4, 5, 6 June 1952

Innings: 1; Not out: 0; Runs: 16; Highest score: 16; Caught: 1; Wickets: 0; Best bowling: 0-86

*Match drawn. Batting first, Worcestershire were dismissed for 229, with only Laddie Outschoorn (68) making a score of note. Batting at number nine John Spilsbury was caught by David Heath off Ray Carter for 16.*

*In reply, the Combined Services amassed 548-4 declared, with centuries from David Heath (149), John Manners (103) and Jim Parks (103 not out). For good measure, there were half-centuries from Alan Shirreff (54) and Robert Wilson (67).*

*Spilsbury bowled 15 overs for 86 runs and played a part in dismissing Manners when he caught him off Norman Whiting's bowling.*

*Worcestershire closed their second innings on 168-3, with half-centuries from Don Kenyon (51) and Outschoorn (54) as the game ended in a draw.*

*Lloyd Rudge was also making his debut for Worcestershire in this game and features elsewhere in this publication.*

Sporting excellence ran through Spilsbury's family. His grandfather, Fred Wheldon, had played in Worcestershire's inaugural first-class match against Yorkshire in 1899 (top-scoring with 49 not out in Worcestershire's first innings) and had an outstanding football career with Aston Villa. He played in their League and FA Cup double winning side of 1896–97. He was capped four times by England and scored a hat-trick on his international debut against Ireland at Trent Bridge in 1897.

*Fred Wheldon wearing his Worcestershire cap.*

John Spilsbury lived in the Farrier's Arms in Worcester, which had been in the family since Fred Wheldon bought it in the early 1900s, and went to St Nicholas' School then to St Martin's School where, in 1945, football and cricket teams were organised.

Spilsbury played his first ever football match against Samuel Southall School.

As a 15-year-old, he played cricket for Milkmaid Sports and Worcester City seconds, who played on the County Ground when the first XI were away. Spilsbury's prowess as a footballer was recognised in 1948, when he played his first match for Worcester City A in the Worcester First Division. By 1950 he had played his first match for Worcester City Reserves in the Birmingham League.

*Worcestershire Schoolboys versus Gloucestershire Schoolboys, 1948-49 season. Spilsbury is standing, second from the right.*

Spilsbury was now studying a five-year apprentice engineering course at the Technical College in Worcester. On 19 April 1952 he had the distinction of playing international football for England's under-18 team against Ireland in Belfast. They lost 2-0.

In June he made his first-class cricket debut for Worcestershire against the Combined Services. In a letter I received from him in 2001 he stated that he remembered the game *'as if it was yesterday'*. He added: *'Lloyd (Rudge) and I arrived early and were shown to the dressing room. As players came in, they looked at us and a few nodded and that was it. Luckily, we both knew Martin Horton who was local and our age. We won the toss and were batting so the three of us went outside to watch. We were all nervous and waited to be told when to pad up. At least I managed to get 16.*

*Spilsbury in football strip.*

'*The next day they batted and took us apart. The wicket was on the edge of the square and in the end, they were hooking from outside off stump to midwicket for six. I was fielding at cover-point and never stopped running all day. My feet were killing me and I was shattered.*

'*The third day was the best. We all felt more comfortable, knew a few more of the players and it rained all day, giving my feet a rest. More importantly we played cards for most of the day and I won!*'

On his return to work at the Midlands Electricity Board (MEB) he expected to be congratulated but instead was told to report to the manager. Recounting that Spilsbury had had time off in the winter to play football and in the summer to play cricket, the manager told him: '*You are an apprentice engineer. Make your mind up! You're either going to be an engineer, a footballer or a cricketer but you can't be all three.*' John left and confessed to being stumped; at that point he decided his future was as an engineer.

Spilsbury was unable to do his national service on account of his poor hearing. Nonetheless, he continued to play his sport to a high standard.

*Cricket match, 24 September, 1952 to celebrate the installation of Worcester City's new floodlights. The sides comprised Worcestershire CCC players, Worcester City CC players and Worcester City FC players. Spilsbury is pictured third from the left on the back row.*

Undeterred, Spilsbury continued to play football and had trials with Stoke City. They offered him terms to sign professionally and stated that he could complete his engineering training in Stoke. He spent a week there attending training and living in a hotel but, having never been away from home before, was happy when Worcester City offered the same terms enabling to sign for them. Another influencing factor was that he was courting Jean Fortey and was concerned that living in Stoke for six days a week would mean he could not see her. They married in 1955 and had a son and two daughters. Spilsbury now has six grandchildren and one great-granddaughter.

After leaving the MEB he went to work in the technical drawing office of Heenan and Froude Ltd. A move to Worcester Heat Systems followed where he worked as the stores' manager until he retired.

One of his most treasured moments in football was playing in an FA Cup tie against Aldershot in the 1957-58 season. He said: *'Having drawn twice, the second replay was played at St Andrews, the home of Birmingham City.*

*'It was the most memorable match for me. 23,000 people were watching, we should have scored early on but we ended up losing 4-2 after extra time. I remember coming up the tunnel. I'd never heard a roar like it before. It was a complete blur for me, but I was amazed by the whole occasion.'*

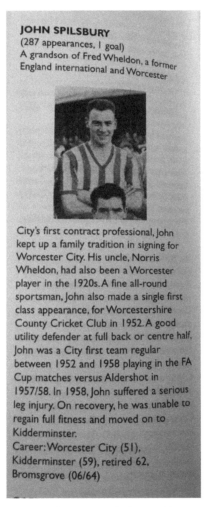

**JOHN SPILSBURY**
(287 appearances, 1 goal)
A grandson of Fred Wheldon, a former England international and Worcester

City's first contract professional, John kept up a family tradition in signing for Worcester City. His uncle, Norris Wheldon, had also been a Worcester player in the 1920s. A fine all-round sportsman, John also made a single first class appearance, for Worcestershire County Cricket Club in 1952. A good utility defender at full back or centre half, John was a City first team regular between 1952 and 1958 playing in the FA Cup matches versus Aldershot in 1957/58. In 1958, John suffered a serious leg injury. On recovery, he was unable to regain full fitness and moved on to Kidderminster.
Career: Worcester City (51), Kidderminster (59), retired 62, Bromsgrove (06/64)

*Synopsis of Spilsbury's football career.*

In the 1958–59 season Worcester City embarked on an FA Cup run which saw them beat Liverpool 2-1 in the third round.

Tragically for Spilsbury bad breaks to the tibia and fibula in his lower leg a few months before meant he missed the Cup run. Nonetheless, the *Daily Mail* visited him in hospital to take pictures of him recuperating while listening to the Liverpool game on the radio. He found the whole episode amusing because they turned up only to find that the game had been postponed and re-arranged for a few days later. They did, though, take the pictures and used them when the game was eventually played.

Spilsbury prided himself on his fitness and at one stage played over 100 consecutive games for Worcester City. His injury prevented him from regaining full fitness and did not play again until 1960. It signalled the end of his time with his beloved Worcester City, which was followed by a move to Kidderminster Harriers where he ultimately became player-manager. He was also a top squash player in the local premier league and had a reputation for beating players 20 years younger. In later life he enjoyed golf and bowls, which allowed him to maintain his competitive sporting edge.

# TASKER

## ALFRED GEORGE ERNEST TASKER – RIGHT-HAND BAT, WICKET-KEEPER

Born: Southwark, London, 16 June 1934
Died: Bentleigh, Victoria, Australia, 18 April 2019

*Portrait of Alf Tasker leaving the pavilion at Lord's.*

First-class matches for Worcestershire: 1 versus Cambridge University, New Road, Worcester, 20, 21, 22 June 1956

Innings: Did not bat; Catches: 1; Stumpings: 0; Did not bowl

*Match drawn. Worcestershire declared their first innings on 349-5 with Laddie Outschoorn scoring 112 and there were half-centuries from Bob Broadbent (68) and 'Dick' Richardson (82 not out).*

*In reply, Cambridge were bowled out for 346 with half-centuries from Ted Dexter (61), John Pretlove (59) and Swaranjit Singh (58). For Worcestershire, acting captain Roly Jenkins took 5-85.*

*Declaring their second innings on 241-4, Don Kenyon scored 116 and Martin Horton 79 not out. Leaving the visitors 245 to win, they closed on 210-8 with Pretlove scoring a second half-century (55). Tasker's contribution was a catch off John Aldridge to dismiss opener Bob Barber for eight.*

Tasker was educated at William Ellis Grammar School at Highgate in London where he played for the school cricket team, leaving in 1950. He played cricket for Wembley Park CC, a club he kept in contact with throughout his life.

His skill as a cricketer was recognised and he was invited to join the MCC ground staff, where he met lifelong friend Tony Pullinger. Pullinger played alongside Tasker in Club and Ground fixtures for Worcestershire and together they embarked on national service, joined the RAF and spent three years stationed in Gloucestershire during which time they continued to play cricket.

*Tasker, extreme left, playing for MCC ground staff.*

Tasker played for Worcestershire Club and Ground XI before he made his first appearance for Worcestershire's second XI on 18 June 1956, in a drawn, two-day game, versus Gloucestershire at The Bottoms in Pershore. The following day he made his first-class debut in the game against Cambridge University and, returning to the seconds three days later, scored a creditable second-innings 49, taking two catches plus one stumping against Warwickshire.

*Worcestershire Club and Ground XI in 1956. Tasker is standing third from the left. Others who feature elsewhere in this publication are: John Chadd (front row, extreme left); Brian Hall (front row, extreme right) and Ron Jones (standing, second from the right).*

On 27 June he was selected to play for a Worcestershire XI against the RAF at New Road. In a letter I received from him in 2001, he referred to two encounters with umpire Dai Davies which he described as 'being initiated' by him.

'*I was keeping wicket and he would pretend that the over was complete after just five balls and move away to square leg. I would begin walking down the wicket towards the other end, whereupon he would return to his post having a laugh at my expense.*

'*On the second day we were in trouble and I came out to bat in the lower order. He remarked in a loud voice that: "the game*

*will soon be over and I will be able to catch the early train home".*
*I then proceeded to bat for about two hours for 21 not out. Raman*
*Subba Row tried bowling donkey drops to encourage me to hit*
*out but I just kept putting the dead bat on them. It was not*
*pretty to watch but I was determined that Mr Davies would*
*miss his train!'*

Tasker signed off with a frank assessment of his time in the
professional game. *'Much as I was disappointed to leave, it was*
*the best thing for me as I realised it would be difficult to earn*
*a living from the game. I then commenced a career in sales and*
*marketing.'* He worked for the Beecham Company in Middlesex
as a sales rep.

*Tasker, batting, showing great concentration.*

In 1965 he emigrated to Australia and met Margaret Gregory,
his future wife, on the boat trip. She described them as 'the £10

poms' – the £10 fee was required to emigrate to Australia. Arriving in Melbourne they were required to stay in Australia for two years where they intended to travel and work, and in Tasker's case play cricket before returning to the UK. He travelled for a while, keeping his promise to maintain contact with Margaret and they married later that year.

He continued to work for the Beecham Company and went to college to study subjects he felt would be useful when he returned home. He played, coached and captained his local team, Highett CC, helping them to win the Victorian Senior League, Second Division title in 1968–69.

In the early 1970s the intended return to the UK was put on hold as Margaret was pregnant. They did eventually make the trip, but, finding it difficult to secure work, returned to Australia. They were to have three sons.

Remaining in the sales environment, Tasker worked for Seager Evans the wine and spirits company, where he acquired expert knowledge of the whisky trade. His last company was an import tool company where he was sales and purchasing manager, buying for the whole of Australia. It necessitated travelling interstate and overseas, a role, despite being demanding, he enjoyed very much. When the company was sold, he decided to retire.

In retirement he joined Yarra Yarra Golf Club playing three times a week. His other hobby was working with Toastmaster International, which he had initially embarked on in 1964. He thrived on the competitions he entered and won them on the international stage when representing Australia.

In 2005 Tasker attended a dinner in the Long Room at Lord's for former members of the MCC ground staff and was reunited with his lifelong friend and former sports master at the Dragon School in Oxford, Tony Pullinger.

*Highett CC in 1968–69. Tasker is on the back row, third from the right.*

*Tasker attending a family function.*

In a recent email, Tasker's son Bradley summed up his father's character, which encompasses the reason for me writing this book: *'He was a good man and his passion for cricket was unparalleled! I'm glad he gets immortalised in your book; he deserves it.'*

# TAYLOR

## ROBERT JOSEPH TAYLOR – RIGHT-HAND BAT, RIGHT-ARM MEDIUM

Born: Liverpool, Lancashire, 1 November 1873
Died: unknown

*Portrait of Robert Taylor.*

First-class matches for Worcestershire: 1 versus London County, Crystal Palace Park, Crystal Palace, 13, 14, 15 August 1900

Innings: 2; Not out: 0; Runs: 1; Highest score: 1; Caught: 0; Wickets: 0; Best bowling: 0-15

*London County won by 166 runs. Winning the toss and batting, London County were dismissed for 345 with Ted Dillon scoring 108. There were half-centuries for George Beldam (67) and the 'grand old man of cricket', W.G. Grace (72). Taylor bowled eight overs which cost him 15 runs.*

*In reply Worcestershire were bowled out for 208 with William Lowe (75) making the only noteworthy score of the innings. Taylor was bowled for one by Len Braund, who finished with 6-78.*

*London County declared their second innings on 206-4 thanks to 110 not out from Grace. Taylor was again wicketless, bowling 12 overs for 26 runs.*

*Set 344 for victory, the visitors were dismissed for 177, with embarrassment being prevented due to 55 from Ted Arnold and 67 from Fred Wheldon. Taylor was caught by Nigel Harrison off Samuel Coe's bowling without score.*

Born in Liverpool to parents, Ann and John Taylor, Robert Taylor played his first representative game of cricket for Lancashire second XI on 17th June 1897, against Surrey at The Oval. He could not have made a better start, taking 7-83 (bowling five ball overs) in a drawn game.

In June the following year, he made one appearance for Lancashire A and followed this with his first-class debut for Lancashire against Surrey at Old Trafford. He was dismissed without score and took just one wicket, that of Fred Holland for 126. In his second and last game for Lancashire he took the wicket of Middlesex's Gregor MacGregor who was caught by England Test batsman Johnny Tyldesley, whose great-great nephew, Michael Vaughan, captained England.

By 1900 Taylor was playing as professional for Kidderminster in the Birmingham League and working locally as a boot maker. He was living in Chester Road, adjacent to the ground, and was married to Lillie Maffey. Their daughter (also named Lillie) was born two years earlier.

The new law of six-ball overs was introduced for the start of the season and in the opening game against Walsall – described as his 'trial game' – Taylor was under the watchful eye of Worcestershire secretary Paul Foley. The match report stated that: *'Mr Foley was a very keen and interested spectator, while Taylor was bowling, eyeing him very carefully with the aid of field glasses. Taylor has signed for a definite period for Worcestershire and will be for two seasons with Kidderminster while he qualifies for the County.'*

Taylor took 3-57 from 27 overs as Kidderminster, chasing 164 to win, hung on for the draw, closing on 96-6. He continued to impress throughout the season, taking three five-wicket hauls, with a best of 6-45 in a nine-wicket win against Aston Unity in May.

He progressed to the Worcestershire's Club and Ground XI in June when he took 2-21 against Shropshire at the County Ground, Frankwell, in Shrewsbury. A week later, in the return fixture at New Road, he claimed a further three wickets in the drawn game. He appeared for Worcestershire's first XI in August which turned out to be his final game of first-class cricket and made one further appearance for the Club and Ground XI against Shropshire in July the following year.

*Lord Graham's Ground in 1909.*

From 1905 until the start of World War One Taylor was employed as cricket professional by, and lived on the estate of, James, Marquis of Graham (6th Duke of Montrose, from 1925) of Easton Park, Woodbridge in Suffolk. Graham's Easton Ramblers side hosted teams at his Easton Park Estate as well as at other venues. Graham is known for taking the first film of a solar eclipse and is credited with inventing the aircraft carrier! When Easton Cricket Club was formed in 1906, Taylor played as their professional.

Between June 1906 and June 1907 Taylor played for Suffolk in the Minor Counties Championship. In June 1906, in the game against Staffordshire at Stoke-on-Trent, he took 3-63 including the wicket of Sydney Barnes for 30 as the game ended in a draw. In August, Barnes was to get his revenge when, in the return fixture at the Town Ground in Felixstowe, he claimed 6-21 and 8-51 – bowling unchanged in both innings – as Staffordshire won by an innings and 164 runs.

*Picture from 1910 from one of Lord Graham's Easton Ramblers games. Taylor is seated on the ground to the right.*

In 1920 Taylor and his wife took up the posts of club steward and stewardess at the Astley Institute for Potential Jockeys at Lisburn Road in Newmarket. He was referred to as the 'Master of Astley Institute' and worked there until his retirement in 1947.

Sir John Dugdale Astley's greatest love was horse racing, and, with his addiction to gambling, he often risked large sums of money with the result that he alternated between the extremes of comparative wealth and poverty.

His love of horses and racing was accompanied by an honest and benevolent nature, and in his later years he used his considerable influence to help others, especially the young men employed in racing. Known as 'The Mate' the Institute was opened in his honour in 1893, just 12 months before he died.

*The Astley Institute circa 1895.*

*Taylor at the Astley Institute for potential jockeys in 1940.*

# THOMAS

## WILLIAM RICHARD KEAY THOMAS – RIGHT-HAND BAT, RIGHT-ARM MEDIUM

Born: Redditch, Worcestershire, 22 July 1960

*Portrait of Will Thomas.*

First-class matches for Worcestershire: 1 versus Sri Lankans, New Road, Worcester, 1, 2, 3 July 1981

Innings: 2; Not out: 1; Runs: 57; Highest score: 44; Caught: 0; Wickets: 0; Best bowling: 0-54

*Match drawn. Worcestershire were dismissed for 301 in their first innings with four batsmen scoring 40s. Batting at number eight, Thomas scored 44 as Somachandra de Silva took 6-100.*

*Batting slowly, the visitors were bowled out for 350 with half-centuiries for Sidath Wettimuny (89) and Duleep Mendis (66). Thomas bowled 17 overs for 54 runs as Dipak Patel, the pick of the bowlers, took 5-76.*

*Due to bad weather and insufficient time to complete the game, Worcestershire's second innings became no more than batting practice, with Mark Scott (73) and Patel (72) making good use of their time at the crease. Thomas finished on 13 not out as the innings closed on 225-6.*

Cricket ran in the Thomas family. Will Thomas's father, Dick, was a committee member at New Road from 1953 until 1986, representing Redditch as a delegate to the General Committee. He ran benefit seasons for Tom Graveney and Basil D'Oliveira and was instrumental in organising many overseas tours. He knew the players from around the country; his pub, The Red Hart at Flyford Flavell, proving to be a popular meeting point. It was a favourite watering hole of David Gower and was also popular with the Sussex team, who would call in whenever they were travelling through the area. Dick would always host a night whenever the tourists were playing at New Road; they were legendary evenings.

One of Thomas's earliest recollections of the New Road ground was playing cricket in the shadow of the chestnut trees with boyhood friend Damian D'Oliveira. In a conversation with Thomas in the summer of 2020 he told me: *'even then, both of us had a close connection to the Club'.*

When Thomas left Dean Close School in Cheltenham in 1978 (where he played in the same team as Tim Graveney, son of Worcestershire great Tom Graveney), he joined Redditch CC and completed a pub management course with the option to go into the trade with his father.

In February 1980 he went on a private tour with Don Lowe's team (The Kingfishers) to Cape Town, the side containing experienced players such as wicket-keeper, Arnold Long. They played at the big venues like Newlands; Thomas was to tour with them again the following year.

He made his first appearance for Worcestershire's Club and Ground XI in early July 1980 and was part of the Warwick Pool under-25 team which lost to Glamorgan at New Road by 56 runs. During the remainder of the summer, he played 14 games for the seconds with three performances of special note. On 4 June he scored 52 not out in the drawn game with Somerset at Taunton, in the process sharing an eighth-wicket partnership of 55 with Vanburn Holder.

Despite a five-wicket defeat at the hands of Yorkshire at Harrogate in early July he finished with 7-72 including the wicket of Martyn Moxon for five. The game at the War Memorial Ground, Amblecote, Stourbridge in mid-July provided great entertainment. Warwickshire declared their second innings on 46-2 leaving Worcestershire 184 to win. Thomas held the innings together with 73, but it was not quite enough as Worcestershire lost by a single run.

In October 1980, as part of Worcestershire's Benefit 80 initiative to raise funds for the Club, he was invited to tour the West Indies, travelling as an amateur. He told me: '*It was great fun to tour with John Inchmore, Barry Jones, Steve Henderson and Paul Fisher.*' Wolverhampton's *Express & Star* newspaper ran the headline – 'Caribbean Carnival for Worcestershire' – nearly 10,000 spectators paid over $20,000 to see the first floodlit game in Barbados.

*He continued: 'The tickets were printed in the USA to prevent local forgeries; it was that much of a hot ticket. The game was played under John Player League rules, with Collis King and Roy Fredericks guesting for us. We won five games in a six-match series.'* The Barbados Invitation XI scored 250-7 with Worcestershire making 251-7 off 38.2 overs.

*'The game was played with a white ball, and Worcestershire played in blue kit and Barbados in gold. Jim Cumbes had to*

*come off at one stage because of the intense heat, so I took over from him.'*

Thomas returned briefly to the UK then flew to Perth to play club cricket in Western Australia. After two net sessions he was told that: *'we don't want a young Pommie'*, so he left to spend time in South Western Australia with his sister, who had married a sheep farmer, and found work there.

During that winter, however, he was diagnosed with toxocariasis, a complaint which attacks the optic nerve and is caught from dogs if they have not been wormed. It manifested itself as a line across his left eye. Returning to England, he saw a specialist in Edgbaston and was then referred to a tropical disease specialist. If untreated, the disease can cause blindness.

He was told not to undertake strenuous exercise and not to play cricket for 12 months, but he still reported back to the County for the 1981 season. He played, but told me that doing so with a permanently dilated pupil made it hard to judge the ball.

*Worcestershire CCC in 1981. Thomas is standing, fourth from the left.*

He played three further second XI games in 1981 before the call-up for the Sri Lanka game in July. He said that Worcestershire were seen at the time as the 'poor relation' compared with other counties, telling me that his one lasting memory of the game was trying to acquire a Club sweater, which proved to be a major event: *'The Club had to beg, steal or borrow them. I got one in the end but it was obviously second hand as it was frayed at the bottom.'*

The year 1981 was an Ashes summer and before the tourists' game at Worcester starting on 25 July the Australians had customarily been wined and dined at the Red Hart. This, too, provided a happy memory for Thomas, as next day he did 12th man duties for the visitors. While batting, Kim Hughes asked for a lemon squash and, still slightly fragile form the night before, was presented with a gin and bitter lemon in a pint glass with the instructions to 'knock it back'. Much to Thomas's surprise and admiration he carried out the order.

Disappointingly, Thomas was released at the end of 1981 and, despite being given a letter saying he was to be offered a contract, was told that he 'was not going to make it'. Reflecting on this, he said that despite the disappointment he much rather enjoyed playing as an amateur, as the professionals had a lot more hassle to contend with.

He started work in 1982 as a financial services rep for Sun Life of Canada and worked for their brokerage in Kenilworth. Married to Jane Phelps in 1987, he later moved to Bain Dawes in Birmingham, working there for 18 years before joining Jardine's as regional director. This necessitated working in Barcelona and Madrid for 18 months.

When in the UK he played for Evesham CC alongside former Worcestershire players Kevin Griffith and Bob Lanchbury. He moved to Ombersley CC before retiring from cricket in his mid-40s.

He recalled taking 10-58 against Stourport in 1997 and scoring 226 versus Hagley. '*I struck two sixes which hit the roof of Hagley Church, which interrupted a wedding ceremony as I broke two roof tiles. It turned out well as I was presented with the tiles as a memento after the game.*'

He is now a keen golfer and has set up a franchise working in business improvement and profit re-engineering, and for the last five years has been with Liaison Group which works alongside the NHS to improve efficiency and profitability.

*Picture of Thomas in 2019.*

# THORNYCROFT

## GUY MYTTON THORNYCROFT – RIGHT-HAND BAT

Born: Blawith, Grange-over-Sands, Lancashire, 1 April 1917
Died: Reading, Berkshire, 8 January 1999

*Portrait of Guy Thornycroft.*

First-class matches for Worcestershire: 1 versus Combined Services, Racecourse Ground, Hereford, 14, 16, 17 June 1947

Innings: 2; Not out: 0; Runs: 3; Highest score: 3; Caught: 0; Did not bowl

*Combined Services won by 131 runs. Combined Services were bowled out in their first innings for 87, with Roly Jenkins (5-41) and Dick Howorth (5-13) sharing the wickets.*

*Worcestershire replied with 110, Thornycroft being bowled by John Whitehead for nought. (Whitehead played 33 matches for Worcestershire between 1953 and 1955.)*

*In their second innings, the visitors made 238 which left Worcestershire 216 to win. They were dismissed for 84 in 27.5, with Thoryncroft run out for three. Whitehead took 5-10 and twice picked up two wickets in two balls.*

In their book, *Cricket in Herefordshire in the Twentieth Century*, Ken Hook and Frank Bennett state that: '*Guy Thornycroft was weaned on cricket by his father, Lieutenant-Colonel Charles Thornycroft.'* This proved to be the case as over a 40-year period Guy played for sides throughout Herefordshire and Shropshire and supported the game at a local level with great vigour.

He was educated at Shrewsbury School, excelled at rugby, football and hockey, and played for the Cricket first XI which in 1933 included 'Sandy' Singleton. Singleton played for Worcestershire from 1934 until 1946 and was captain in his final season. In the drawn game against Malvern in 1934, Thornycroft scored 134 and the following season finished with 500 runs from just 12 innings with a top score of 130. In the review of the school's season, *The Cricketer Annual* stated: *'G.M. Thornycroft proved a fine, attacking batsman.'* The same season he began a long association with the Gentlemen of Herefordshire. He also represented the Gentlemen of Shropshire.

In July 1938, while playing for the Grasshoppers against the Dinkie Doodles in a Leominster Senior Divisional knockout match, he made a rapid 46 not out (including three sixes and five fours) and then took 5-19 as the Grasshoppers won by 91 runs.

After passing out from the Royal Military Academy at Sandhurst, in 1937, Second Lieutenant Guy Thornycroft joined the 2nd Battalion of the King's Shropshire Light Infantry (KSLI) and served the regiment with distinction during the War. Sadly, two of his brothers, John and Charles, were to lose their lives. His other brother, Nigel, was held in a Gestapo prisoner of war camp and in 1955 published a book, *Fowlers Moon*, recounting his childhood days in rural Herefordshire. He later moved to Rhodesia where he ran a tobacco, game and cattle farm, naming it 'Merrhill' after the wood in Herefordshire which he remembered with such fondness.

Whenever he could during the War, Guy arranged for cricket coaching to take place at Hereford Racecourse and helped raise considerable amounts of money for many War-related charities.

He also organised cricket matches between his own XI and local military sides to help improve the morale of the troops in the area. Included in his side was Reg Perks who played for Worcestershire from 1930 until 1955 and was the Club's first professional captain in his final season.

By 1943 Thornycroft had been promoted to lieutenant and during the D-Day landings commanded a company of the KSLI landing on Sword Beach. Official records say his leadership and personal courage throughout the campaign earned him the trust and admiration of his men.

In 2002 Private Bill Hollyhead, a radio operator from X Company of the KSLI, who had served with Thornycroft referred to him as '*a very brave leader*'. He was mentioned in despatches in 1944.

*The cricketing Thornycrofts. From left to right: Colonel Charles Thornycroft and his sons Nigel, John, Charles and Guy.*

He continued to lead the company in the advance through Normandy and, after being appointed second in command of the battalion, remained with the troops until they reached the Netherlands. He later served with headquarters, 12th Army in Burma, and HQ Burma Command until 1946. He re-joined the KSLI and served with the regiment in Palestine and the Sudan. His final appointment as a serving officer was colonel of the Light Infantry Brigade.

*Portrait of Guy Thornycroft.*

In 1946, he concentrated on building up local cricket again, writing strong letters to the *Hereford Times* stating that Herefordshire cricket must recommence; he urged local cricketers to start playing again.

On account of his efforts the Hereford Evening League started up again in the summer of 1946. He also sponsored a Hereford six-a-side competition called the Thornycroft Trophy. He was influential in organising Herefordshire Minor County matches plus a one-off match between MCC and the Combined Services.

Prior to his first-class appearance for Worcestershire in 1947 he embraced his appearance by writing to the *Hereford Times* once more, on this occasion asking Hereford cricket enthusiasts to support the match because it was the first, first-class match to be played in Hereford since 1919.

In the spring of 1947 he married Kathleen Evans and during the summer hit 203 against the South Wales Hunt XI, his second hundred coming in less than 30 minutes. His opening partner, Noel Pritchard, said: '*Guy proved himself to be one of the finest attacking batsmen ever seen in Herefordshire. While I compiled a mere 30, he hit 200 with awesome power. One of his towering sixes put the ball through the windscreen of a car belonging to a member of the team who had only bought it that day. He also hit one ball over the old grandstand of the racecourse. Only those who saw this feat would consider it possible.*'

In February 1954 he was appointed commanding officer of the 1st Battalion of The Herefordshire Light Infantry. Later he was appointed deputy lieutenant of Shropshire, became the high sheriff in 1975 and was a one-time president of the county's Royal British Legion. The *London Gazette* reported in 1976 his appointment as deputy honorary colonel of the 6th Battalion the Light Infantry (Volunteers).

For many years he lived at Cressage in Shropshire but in the mid 1990's moved to Shinfield, near Reading, where he later died. At the time of his death, his son, Mark, worked for the Forestry Commission and his second son, David, was a colonel in the Black Watch and deputy chief of staff at Headquarters 5th Division at Copthorne Barracks, Shrewsbury, his father's regimental home.

Guy's influence across Herefordshire and Shropshire is still evident today. In 1987 Guy Thornycroft Court – a complex of retirement homes – was built in Ludlow, Shropshire, in recognition of his lifelong service to the local community.

# TIPPER

**BENJAMIN CLAUDE CECIL TIPPER – RIGHT-HAND BATSMAN, BOWLING ACTION UNKNOWN, OCCASIONAL WICKET-KEEPER**

Born: King's Norton, Worcestershire, 7 July 1896
Died: Norton Lindsey, Warwickshire, 11 July 1970

*Portrait of Cecil Tipper.*

First-class matches for Worcestershire: 5
- Versus Gloucestershire, New Road, Worcester, 23, 24 June 1919
- Versus Somerset, New Road, Worcester, 7, 8 July 1919
- Versus H.K. Foster's XI, Racecourse Ground, Hereford, 14, 15 July 1919
- Versus Gloucestershire, College Ground, Cheltenham, 18, 19 August 1919
- Versus Warwickshire, New Road, Worcester, 25, 26 August 1919

Innings: 10; Not out: 1; Runs: 137; Highest score: 43; Caught: 7; Wickets: 4; Best bowling: 2-0

Against Gloucestershire #1, match drawn. *Worcestershire were dismissed for 201 with a half-century for Thomas Allchurch (51);*

Tipper made 42 before becoming one of Francis Ellis's four victims.

Gloucestershire replied with 334 thanks to Harry Huggins (92), Philip Williams (59) and Harry Smith (74). Tipper took 2-49 from 15 overs. In their second innings Worcestershire declared on 282-9 with half-centuries from Cecil Turner (72), Fred Bowley (50) and Maurice Jewell (84). Needing 150 to win, Gloucestershire closed on 109-4 with Foster Robinson contributing 62.

Geoffrey Sheppard was also making his debut in this game and features elsewhere in this publication.

Against Somerset, match drawn. Worcestershire dismissed Somerset for 172 and replied with 203 thanks to a century from Fred Bowley (101). In their second innings Somerset were bowled out for 240 with scores from Sydney Rippon (73) and Philip Hope (54), which left Worcestershire a target of 210. Closing on 149-8 only a half-century from Bowley (50) staved off a likely defeat.

Against H.K. Foster's XI, H.K. Foster's XI won by four wickets. Worcestershire were dismissed for 87 with Tipper scoring five before falling to Humphrey Gilbert who took 6-50. H.K. Foster's XI were then bowled out for 185 with Frank Phillips scoring 63.

In their second innings, Worcestershire were bowled out for 256, with a half-century for Maurice Jewell (56). Tipper made 24 not out and Gilbert claimed another five wickets (6-72). It left H.K. Foster's side needing 159 for victory. They reached their target for the loss of six wickets with Phillips top-scoring with 92 not out.

Against Gloucestershire #2, match drawn. The visitors were dismissed for 213 with Fred Bowley scoring 101 as Charlie Parker claimed 7-111. Tipper was one of his victims, being bowled for one.

*Gloucestershire replied with 185, Alf Dipper carrying his bat for 99 not out. With eight wickets down, Tipper came on to bowl and took two wickets in two balls to leave Dipper stranded. He caught and bowled Stanley Brown for a duck and bowled Parker with his next delivery. Bad weather intervened as Worcestershire closed on 32-3 to draw the game.*

*Against Warwickshire, match drawn. Worcestershire were all out for 187 with Tipper top-scoring with 43 before falling to Edward Hewetson. Harry Howell finished with 6-69. In reply, Warwickshire were bowled out for 145, with Horace Venn scoring 58, Maurice Jewell taking 7-56 and Tipper claiming four catches.*

*Worcestershire declared their second innings on 102-7 (Tipper 0) thereby setting the visitors 145 to win; they closed on 70-2.*

Cecil Tipper was the eldest child of Claude Nash Tipper and his wife Katie. His childhood was spent at family homes in King's Heath and Moseley in Birmingham. Tipper Snr, ran his own business – B.C. Tipper and Sons – manufacturing animal medicines from his premises in Homer Street, Balsall Heath. Advertisements for the company extolled the virtues of their products including lice powders, cattle purgatives, mystery salts (conditioner and blood purifier) and many other mysterious potions.

Tipper, who had two siblings, Kathleen and Maurice, was educated at King Edward's School in Birmingham where he played cricket for the first XI, which was captained by 'Laddie' Higgins who played 97 matches for Worcestershire between 1920 and 1927.

In 1912, opening the innings, Tipper scored 39 for King Edward's against Jesus College, Oxford and 12 months later against The Oratory School top-scored with 16 out of an innings total of 71. Despite the low total, they dismissed The Oratory School for 55 to win by a narrow margin.

*Tipper's advertisement from 1910.*

In April 1914, playing club cricket for Ashfield CC, a local Birmingham side, he top-scored with 62 not out (out of a total of 142) against Robin Hood at Moorlands, Hall Green. It proved to be match-winning as Robin Hood were dismissed for 91. Tipper had a long association with Ashfield, playing for them until 1941.

Having previously played for Warwickshire's Club and Ground XI, he made his debut for Warwickshire second XI on 1 June 1914 in the 120-run defeat to Derbyshire. It proved unsuccessful, as opening the innings he had scores of nought and three. Two days later, playing for King Edward's, he top-scored with 66 and took 2-41 in a draw with King's School, Worcester. The following week he had the outstanding bowling figures of 6-10 (from 16 overs including 10 maidens) as King Edward's beat Bromsgrove School by 57 runs.

In World War One Tipper served as a second lieutenant in the Worcestershire Regiment, Training Battalion and gazetted as lieutenant in 1917. The same year he married Hilda Smith at Aston in Birmingham; they had three sons, Cecil Edgar (born 1919), Rodney Gerald (born 1923) and John Anthony (born 1926). His youngest son, a sergeant, tragically lost his life at El-Alamein in World War Two.

*Worcestershire side versus Warwickshire at New Road, 1919.*
*Back row, left to right: W. Machell (umpire), F. Bowley, E. Bale,*
*R.D. Burrows, A. Conway, A.N. Jewell, F. Hunt*
*(groundsman and umpire for this game).*
*Front row, left to right: M.F.S. Jewell, W. Taylor, A.T. Cliff, J.W.C. Turner.*
*Tipper is on the ground on the left; H.W. Isaac (who appears elsewhere*
*in this publication) is to the right.*

Tipper's first-class debut for Worcestershire came in their opening game of the 1919 season against Gloucestershire at New Road on 23 June. He was to play four further first-class matches including one against H.K. Foster's XI.

On 27 August Tipper was to make one final appearance in a Worcestershire XI, in a game against MCC at New Road. Ending in a draw he was out 'hit wicket' for 10.

By the early 1920s he once more played games for Warwickshire Club and Ground XI and continued to play for Ashfield. In 1926

265

he began another long association, this time with Warwickshire Imps whom he represented until 1951.

In 1931 he made his sole appearance for the Worcestershire Regiment, against the Gentlemen of Worcestershire. Robert Berkeley, who played four matches for Worcestershire from 1919 until 1922, scored 100 not out for the Gentlemen. In June 1933 the highlight for Tipper was 113 for Ashfield as they beat local side Harborne Somerville by 69 runs.

The census from 1939 shows that Tipper was still involved in the family business. Now living in Park Avenue, Solihull, it states his occupation as managing director, animal medicine and agricultural allied specialities. He continued to make appearances for Ashfield and maintained his long affinity with King Edward's Old Edwardian Association, making his final appearance for them in 1956 – shortly after his 60th birthday – in the annual fixture between the old boys and the school.

*Tipper attending a wedding.*

# VORSTER

## LOUIS PHILLIPPUS VORSTER – LEFT-HAND BAT, RIGHT-ARM OFF-BREAK

Born: Potchefstroom, Transvaal, South Africa, 2 November 1966
Died: Muldersdrift, Gauteng, South Africa, 17 April 2012

*Portrait of Louis Vorster.*

First-class matches for Worcestershire: 1 versus the West Indians, New Road, Worcester, 28, 29, 30 May 1988

Innings: 1; Not out: 1; Runs: 16; Highest score: 16 not out; Caught: 0; Did not bowl

*Batting first, Worcestershire declared on 321-3 thanks to Tim Curtis (82) and Graeme Hick (172). In reaching 154, Hick passed 1,000 first-class runs before the end of May. Vorster was 16 not out when the declaration was made.*

*The Tourists replied with 170-5 with half-centuries for Desmond Haynes (71) and Viv Richards (50). Disappointingly, rain came to spoil a well-poised game.*

Vorster was educated at Potchefstroom High School and Hoër Volkskool in Potchefstroom, where his father was a leading cricket coach. He held a bursary from Rand Afrikaans University, spent time at the University of Pretoria and later the University of Potchefstroom where he obtained his bachelor of arts.

A talented left-handed bat, he was selected to tour England with South Africa Schools in 1983. In November 1985 he made his first-class debut for Transvaal B against Eastern Province B at the Wanderers in Johannesburg. In his next two games his promise was clear to see as he struck 50 against Northern Transvaal B and 51 against Griqualand West. In 1986 he spent time with Halesowen in the Birmingham League and even played a game of rugby for Halesonians Rugby Club fourth XV, following the cancellation of a pre-season cricket match due to bad weather.

During the winter of 1986–87 he had one of his best seasons, scoring 516 runs at an average of 46.90, with a highest score of 74 not out when opening the batting for South Africa Universities against a strong Australian XI. In January 1988 he scored his first, first-class hundred – 174 for Transvaal against Western Province at Newlands.

In May 1987, he played for Warwickshire second XI against MCC Young Cricketers at Edgbaston, scoring 64 and 36 in a drawn game. He returned to the UK for the 1988 summer, playing for Kidderminster in the Birmingham League.

His opportunity for Worcestershire came in mid-May in a second XI game versus Lancashire at Old Trafford when he scored a second innings 101 before being run out. Following his first-class appearance for Worcestershire he then returned to the seconds and played six further games, scoring three half-centuries.

*Vorster in 1988.*

Back in South Africa he represented Transvaal, Northern Transvaal, Northern Transvaal B and North West. A fine season came in 1993–94 when, from six games, he scored 394 runs at an average of 49.25, including two hundreds, with a best of 188 for Northern Transvaal B versus Orange Free State B. In April the following year he played a first-class game for a Matabeleland Invitation XI against Worcestershire, on their pre-season tour to Zimbabwe, scoring 83 before being caught by Stuart Lampitt off Chris Tolley. He retired from cricket in 1998.

He joined Jan Morgan, a Pretoria based businessman and took up a 20 per cent share in a logistics company that would eventually become South Africa's largest logistics company specialising in the airfreight of fresh produce. The firm pioneered a fresh-value chain in Europe which saw it effectively monopolise the industry for many years. It had warehouses in London, Frankfurt and Amsterdam. It later diversified into cattle ranching, feedlots and horticulture, all on a national scale.

In a recent email, his good friend Marco van Niekerk summed up Vorster's approach to his work and gave an insight into his personality: *'Because of his calm personality and reputation for diligence and gentlemanly conduct, clients always preferred to phone Louis personally on his mobile phone instead of dealing with one of the 10 booking agents sitting in the Johannesburg office. Louis must have had a photographic memory because he had the uncanny ability to navigate between hundreds of bookings across dozens of flights all in a split-second without checking electronically.'*

Vorster proceeded to build up a private cattle-ranching enterprise in Namibia to where he eventually moved. He resigned his position with Morgan Cargo and sold his shares in the Morgan Group towards the beginning of 2006, and continued to build his new venture into a significant beef-production enterprise. Surprisingly, he was persuaded out of cricket retirement to play for and captain Namibia in 2007, playing six games for them before retiring for a second time in 2009.

An excellent pilot, he flew a Piper PA-31 Navajo on a professional and recreational basis and remained passionate about cricket. He was a big supporter of developing young, high-potential cricketers, the result being that many of the players we identify with South African cricket today, such as Albie and Morne Morkel, A.B. de Villiers, Faf du Plessis and Dale Steyn, worked with Vorster at Supersport Park in Centurion where he organised strict training and exercise programmes for them.

Van Niekerk shared a house with Vorster and recalls one conversation with de Villiers: *'The players had finished their "beep tests" and while Louis was inside the house A.B. dryly commented that it was particularly embarrassing to have Louis challenge them around their level of fitness and to then prove later on that he outperformed them on the test. Louis had just turned 40 at the time. He was an extremely humble guy, so this was purely done to challenge them to improve.'*

*Vorster at the controls of his plane.*

In April 2012, tragedy struck when Vorster was murdered at a petrol filling station near Pretoria, having been followed from a local bank. He had made a sizeable withdrawal and was intent on buying a generator from a farmer in Krugersdorp and needed cash for the transaction. Information was apparently leaked to a syndicate by one of the bank's employees and Vorster was followed to the station where he was ambushed as he came out of the convenience store. He was shot three times and died at the scene.

Van Niekerk told me: '*Louis was one of the most unselfish people I got to know. He always used to say that he was fortunate to have met so many good people who allowed him the opportunities he had. He was extremely honest and had a reputation for someone you could do a "hand shake deal" with.*'

The final paragraph in the terrible conclusion to this profile is provided by van Niekerk: '*We, Albie Morkel, Jacques Rudolph and I, went to extraordinary lengths to make sure the murderers were tracked down, employing Piet Byleveld, one of the top private investigators in South Africa.*

'*The security team we contracted managed to put together a dossier which was handed to the South African Police, but unfortunately they could never successfully prosecute for reasons which are sadly obvious. When I followed up a few years ago I was informed that the actual shooter was killed in what they call a "cash in transit" heist effectively closing an extremely sad chapter.*'

# WATKINS

## STEPHEN GEORGE WATKINS – RIGHT-HAND BAT, RIGHT-ARM MEDIUM

Born: Hereford, 23 March 1959

*Portrait of Steve Watkins.*

First-class matches for Worcestershire: 1 versus Oxford University, The Parks, Oxford, 15, 16, 17 June 1983

Innings: 2; Not out: 0; Runs: 105; Highest score: 77; Caught: 0; Did not bowl

*Worcestershire won by 148 runs. Having been put in to bat, the visitors declared on 342-8 with Watkins, who opened the batting with Mark Scott (53), scoring 77. David Banks with 100 became only the fourth Worcestershire batsman to score a century on their first-class debut. Harry Rawlinson (5-123) was the pick of the Oxford bowlers.*

*Oxford declared on 285-6 with half-centuries for Richard Ellis (61), Andrew Miller (90) and Roger Moulding (53 not out).*

*Worcestershire declared their second innings on 228-8, with Watkins scoring 28 and half-centuries for Damian D'Oliveira (52)*

*and Banks (53). Requiring 286 to win, Oxford were dismissed for 137 as the wickets were shared between four bowlers.*

A recent e-mail I received from Watkins indicated how much satisfaction he gained from his time at New Road: *'The early 80s was a great time to be involved with Worcestershire. It was a time of transition, Basil D'Oliveira was coach and a number of experienced players like Glenn Turner, Norman Gifford, Alan Ormrod and Ted Hemsley were coming to the end of their careers.*

*'A number of exciting young players came to the fore: Tim Curtis, Phil Newport, Richard Illingworth, Ricardo Ellcock; there were also a number of local players like Damian D'Oliveira, David Banks, Martin Weston and Steve McEwan, plus Peter Moores and Allan Warner, who all went on to strong county careers ... Not to mention a young Graeme Hick and then Phil Neale taking over the captaincy in 1982.'*

Watkins was educated at Lady Hawkins' School in Kington, Herefordshire and then studied at Worcester Technical College where he successfully completed the Association of Accounting Technicians qualification. In addition, he gained a bachelor of science (hons) in sports coaching and development through the University of Wales in Newport. When he joined the staff at Worcestershire in 1982 he was a local government officer with South Hereford Council and was playing for Hereford City Sports Club. In 1977 he had been a member of the team which won the Three Counties League Challenge.

His first game for Worcestershire second XI was against Gloucestershire at Bristol in 1980 and he went on to make six further appearances in 1981. The following season proved to be a memorable one as the talented players he referred to in the opening paragraph matured into a fine team. He hit six half-centuries (with a best of 72 against Nottinghamshire) and finished the season with 649 runs at an average of 30.90.

In the final game against Warwickshire at Moseley, Worcestershire needed a win to be crowned champions. Ricardo Ellcock took 7-46 as the home side were dismissed for 121, with Worcestershire indebted to Mark Scott with 97 as they replied with 286. Dismissed in their second innings for 260 (Neal Abberley 107 not out), Warwickshire set Worcestershire 96 to win.

The report of the game in Worcestershire's 1983 yearbook stated: '*At 6-1 Worcestershire were looking nervous. Bryan Jones joined Steve Watkins and if they had any doubts about the result, they hid them masterfully with a manner which oozed authority and self-assurance.*' Jones (the brother of Barry Jones who played for Worcestershire from 1976 until 1980) finished on 50 not out and Watkins on 31 not out to secure a nine-wicket victory and the title.

*Second XI champions, 1982.*
*Back row, left to right: Basil D'Oliveira (coach), Allan Warner, Richard Illingworth, Steve Watkins, Peter Moores, David Banks, Phil Newport, Ricardo Ellcock, Darren Shorter, Paul Wintle (scorer).*
*Front row, left to right: Steve Perryman, Martin Weston, Tim Curtis, Mark Scott, Andy Webster, Damian D'Oliveira.*

Watkins's first-class debut came at Oxford in June the following year; he commented: '*I opened with Mark Scott and put on 122. I should have got a hundred but I nicked a wide one. David Banks scored a century, hitting a six over the pavilion, many claiming it to be the biggest ever hit on the ground!'*

He was included in the squad to play in the Championship game against Kent at Canterbury in early August but the late availability of Tim Curtis meant that he was omitted. He did, though, play in the John Player Sunday League game and remembers it vividly: *'There were 4,000 Kent supporters packed in and I was fielding under the lime tree. A strong Kent side batted first and were in trouble at 50-3, but Chris Cowdrey scored 95. I dropped a skier off him under the tree when he was on 64. I opened with Dipak Patel and made 24 (joint top score with David Humphries) and hit Richard Ellison for six over square leg. I was out caught Knott bowled Woolmer, having top edged a pull, Knott running back towards fine leg to take the catch.'*

Later in the month he was in the side which lost the Warwick Pool Under-25 Final to Leicestershire. With the scores level on 198, Leicestershire were judged the winners as they had lost fewer wickets (five compared with Worcestershire's eight). A copy of the team picture can be found in Harshad Patel's profile.

Leaving at the end of the season, Watkins played Birmingham League cricket for Worcester City CC for three years before moving to South Wales as a semi-professional with Croesyceiliog CC, where he stayed for 12 successful seasons.

They won the Gwent League title and cup, progressing into the South Wales Alliance and eventually into the South East Wales League. In 1988, while working as an accountant for South Herefordshire District Council, Watkins also played for Wales Minor Counties (Wales MC) in their first ever Minor Counties game at Christ Church, Oxford, against Oxfordshire.

In 1991 they played a strong West Indies side at Brecon, the team including Viv Richards, Richie Richardson, Carl Hooper and

Jeff Dujon. The West Indies made 362-6 off 55 overs. Watkins picking up Brian Lara's wicket when he was stumped by Adrian Shaw for 82. He recalled: *'Carl Hooper (88) and Lara were majestic and hit the ball many a mile. I opened and made just three before edging a rising Patrick Patterson delivery into Dujon's gloves about 30 yards back; but it was a fantastic day and one not to be forgotten.'*

He made the move to Herefordshire in 1992, to play in their inaugural season in the Minor Counties Championship. *'The opening game against Wales MC was memorable in that we were totally outplayed until the last session when we were set 266 in 51 overs to win. We got home off the last ball by five wickets, with Watkins 70, Jeremy Leighton 70 and Matthew Robinson 64 not out.'*

*The victorious Herefordshire side.*
*Watkins is on the front row, second from the right.*

He played his final Championship game against Devon at Exmouth the following year, signing off in style by scoring 76 and 65 in a drawn game.

In 1999 he left Herefordshire Council and took up the post of cricket development officer for the Cricket Board of Wales, where he worked until 2016. During that time, in 2010, he played three games for Wales over-50s.

The role included running the National Development Centre at Newport and the Wales under-12 national team. He said he had the privilege of working alongside ex-Glamorgan players Tom Cartwright, Allan Jones, Barry Lloyd and John Derrick plus Somerset's Graham Burgess.

*'It was gratifying to work with so many young players who went on to play first-class cricket, such as David Lloyd, Andrew Salter, Prem Sisodiya, Ruaidhri Smith and Tom Maynard. For the Wales under-12s, the annual tournament at Ampleforth College – run by Don Wilson, ex-Yorkshire and England – was always the highlight of the season, especially playing against the likes of Jonny Bairstow, Adam Lyth and Andrew Gale.'*

In 2016 he was appointed director of operations at Herefordshire Cricket to oversee all cricket from club level to junior age groups and National Counties. He firmly hopes that he will help to produce more local players who represent Herefordshire and maybe one day Worcestershire and England.

*Watkins in 2016, having being appointed to his role with Herefordshire.*

# WINNINGTON

## JOHN FRANCIS SARTORIUS WINNINGTON – RIGHT-HAND BAT

Born: Charlton Kings, Gloucestershire, 17 September 1876
Died: (in action) near Kefar Kassin, Ramle, Palestine, 22 September 1918

*Portrait of John Winnington.*

First-class matches for Worcestershire: 1 versus Oxford University, The Parks, Oxford, 11, 12, 13 June 1908.

Innings: 2; Not out: 0; Runs: 20; Highest score: 20; Caught: 0; Did not bowl

*Worcestershire won by 332 runs. In the first innings Worcestershire were indebted to George Simpson-Hayward who, out of a total of 185, scored 105 in just 80 minutes.*

*Batting at number ten Winnington was dismissed without score, being caught by Malcolm Salter off the bowling of Humphrey Gilbert who finished with 5-54. Gilbert went on to play 72 matches for Worcestershire between 1921 and 1930.*

*Simpson-Hayward continued his excellent form and took 6-13 in the University's first innings of 85. Batting for a second time Worcestershire scored 362, William Burns striking 146 (in just over two hours at the crease). On this occasion, Winnington scored 20, with Gilbert taking 6-170. Leaving Oxford 463 to win, all-rounder Ted Arnold made light work of their second innings claiming 7-51 as Oxford were dismissed for 130.*

*Guy Pawson, Freddy Grisewood and Eric Brownell were also making their debuts for Worcestershire in this game and feature elsewhere in this publication.*

John Winnington was a career soldier, as was his father, Major John Taylor Winnington, who served with the Dragoon Guards. Educated at Worcester Park, Surrey and the Oxford Military College, John Winnington was commissioned as a second lieutenant into a Militia Battalion of the Worcestershire Regiment on 30 January 1895. He later transferred into the regular Army and joined the 1st Battalion of the Worcesters on 15 March 1897, and found time to play cricket for Norton Barracks, participating in local fixtures against teams such as Stoke Prior and Bromyard.

In the Second Boer War (1899–1902) he fought with the 2nd Battalion of the Royal Dublin Fusiliers up to the relief of Ladysmith, then returning to the 2nd Battalion of the Worcestershire Regiment in the Orange River Colony. He was invalided home with dysentery, but later returned and saw action at Spion Kop, Vaal Kranz and Pieter's Hill. He was awarded the Queen's Medal with four clasps and then promoted to captain on 2 January 1901.

In 1904, he played cricket for the Gentlemen of Worcestershire against MCC at New Road, in a game remembered for a fine 118 not out from Cecil Turner who 'carried his bat'. Turner played for Worcestershire from 1911 until 1921 and was a barrister at the Inner Temple with an expertise in Roman and criminal law. He was a fellow of Trinity Hall, Cambridge and was awarded the Military Cross in January 1918.

Winnington was appointed adjutant to the 5th Battalion Worcestershire Regiment from 1906 until 1910, during which time he made his first-class debut for Worcestershire. On 20 July 1910 he married Joyce Mary Marriage; they were to have two children, Susanne born in 1913 and Mary born in 1917.

He was appointed adjutant to the 1st Battalion in 1912 and promoted to major in 1914 as World War One broke out.

*Major J.F.S. Winnington, front row, second from the right, Cairo, 1914.*

At the battle of Neuve Chapelle in 1915, Winnington led two companies in several attacks, being awarded the Distinguished Service Order for his gallantry; he was also mentioned in despatches for his actions. An extract from the citation reads: '*He showed great foresight in anticipating the desires of the Brigade Commander in regard to the advance of other troops at a time when orders could not be conveyed to them.*' Promoted to lieutenant-colonel for his actions, as well as being awarded his Brevet Colonelcy in the 1915 Birthday Honours for distinguished work, he was, though, invalided home due to the strain and exposure of three successive days and nights of fighting.

Following his recovery he was posted to Gallipoli in 1916, where he was once again mentioned in despatches for his gallant actions. During intense fighting his health broke down once more, however, and he suffered frost-bitten feet and dysentery. He was invalided home and deemed physically unfit for further duty. It was the last time he served with the Worcester Regiment.

He became assistant inspector of recruiting in 1917 and, at Pitchcroft in Worcester, gave drill instruction to the Worcester Volunteer Training Corps and delivered lectures to them on sentry and support duties.

Armed with a token of their thanks – an inscribed silver matchbox 'wishing him God speed and good luck', plus a case of Barling's pipes – he was posted to the 4th Battalion of the Northampton Regiment in Palestine where, tragically, he lost his life in September 1918. In the *Worcestershire Regiment in the Great War* author Captain Henry FitzMaurice Stacke (MC) explained the circumstances surrounding Colonel Winnington's death: '*A stray shell burst at Colonel Winnington's feet and injured him terribly. He lived for a couple of days but then died. He is a very great loss as he was a first-class Commanding Officer, quite one in a hundred who had done a great deal for the Northamptons. I am very sorry indeed that he is gone.*'

Winnington was mentioned in despatches once again, for his actions with the Northamptonshire Regiment, and is commemorated in the Ramleh War Cemetery on the outskirts of Tel-Aviv and on a window in the cloisters of Worcester Cathedral.

*Worcester Cathedral cloisters window commemorating the life of J. F. S. Winnington.*

# PICTURE ACKNOWLEDGEMENTS

Every attempt has been made to seek permission for copyright material used in this book, however, if we have inadvertently used copyright material without permission/acknowledgement we apologise and we will make the necessary correction at the first opportunity.

I would like to acknowledge the following who have either supplied or given their permission for images to be reproduced in this book.

Alamy
Balliol College, Oxford
Barnoldswick Cricket Club
Frank Bennett
Berrow's Worcester Journal
Bradford Telegraph and Argus
Breweryhistory.com
The Chatham family collection
The Charterhouse collection
Christ Church College, Oxford
Corporate Services Department of Planning, Industry and Environment, New South Wales
Coventry and North Warwick Cricket Club
The Cricket Paper/Greenway Publishing
The Davis family collection
Eastbourne Herald
Mary Evans Picture Library
The Foley family collection
Glamorgan County Cricket Club Cricket Archives
The Good family collection
The Goodreds family collection
Grace's Guide to British Industrial History
Hereford Times

Highett Cricket Club
The Tim Jones collection
The Kenyon family collection
Kidderminster Cricket Club
Magdalen College Oxford – images by kind permission
of the President and Fellows of Magdalen College Oxford
Max-books.
The Moule family collection
Judith Murphy/Garth Dawson Studio
Andrew Murtagh
The Pawson family collection
Julian Pugh, Worcester City Football Club
Radley College
Republikein newspaper, Namibia
Gordon Rigg Bradford Premier League
The Rudge family collection
The Mike Scothern collection
Shropshire County Cricket Club
Ian Smith Sports Photography
Redleg - Australian Rules Football Museum
Seen Australia
The Shropshire Star
Stirling Archives
The Tasker family collection
Tasmanian State Library and Archive Service
Sandra Taylor from rememberthefallen.co.uk
The Thornycroft family collection
Trinity Hall, Cambridge
Tonbridge School
Trove: http://nla.gov.au/nla.obj-310953783
Trustees of the Mercian Regiment Museum (Worcestershire)
Marco Van Niekerk
Worceser City Football Club
Worcester News
Worcestershire County Cricket Club heritage collection
World Rugby Museum

Lightning Source UK Ltd.
Milton Keynes UK
UKHW021248200621
385758UK00004B/126/J

9 781839 755842